SWISH FISH

An Entertaining Guide to Buying and Cooking Fish

John Kenward
and
Nicholas Roe

HODDER AND STOUGHTON
London   Sydney   Auckland   Toronto

British Library Cataloguing in Publication Data

Kenward, John
  Swish fish.
  1. Great Britain. Food. Fish
  I. Title   II. Roe, Nicholas
  641.3′92

  ISBN 0-340-49151-5

First published in Great Britain 1989

Published by Hodder and Stoughton,
a division of Hodder and Stoughton Ltd,
Mill Road, Dunton Green, Sevenoaks, Kent TN13 2YJ
Editorial Office: 47 Bedford Square, London WC1B 3DP

Photoset by Litho Link Ltd, Welshpool, Powys, Wales

Printed in Great Britain by T. J. Press (Padstow) Ltd,
Padstow, Cornwall.

CONTENTS

WHITING AND SPRATS
WITH LEEK AND FENNEL

Fifteen seconds is not a lot of time in which to
settle the whole direction of a meal, but it was
raining and we were getting wet.

There were twenty-two varieties of fish laid
out on the fishmonger's slab, just the other side of
the window. That is, twenty-two ways of making a
fool of yourself if you don't know much about
seafood – or twenty-two ways of being undecided
if you do.

The key, said restaurant-owner John
Kenward, who was standing next to me in the
drizzle, was to pick on a single idea and act upon it
at once. Otherwise you could stand there for
hours getting wet like this while the huge weight
of choice gave up being exciting and became
simply oppressive.

"Yes, John," I said. "And what is the single
idea?"

He hesitated for those fifteen seconds and
said, "A contrast of textures." Then he plunged
into the shop and bought half a pound of sprats and
a couple of cheerful-looking whiting – and this
book got under way.

The place was Lewes – the county town of
East Sussex; a beautiful town full of hills, flint
walls and odd lanes, in one of which John runs a
restaurant called Kenwards and where, at the

time, I owned a fish shop (the one we were standing outside).

There was no reason why we had chosen to start a book on this particular day, or with this selection of fish. On the contrary, we had agreed never to be anything else but average shoppers facing everyday shopping problems . . . like shortage of time, small or wide ranges of choice, and rain. Only that way (we reasoned) could we hope to deal with the basic problem of cooking fish, which is the sheer uncertainty of supply.

It's true. Count on being able to buy haddock – because you know a great recipe for haddock – and sure as eggs that is the one fish your monger will not have. Storms will have blown up and the ports will have closed; or perhaps the shop has simply run out. Maybe the fishmonger just did not like the price and refused to buy any. With fish, you have to be prepared to throw plans to the wind (a joke). When that happens, you need to know *ways* of cooking seafood, any seafood. It is not enough just to memorise recipes, you have to be able to relax with the subject and feel at home.

So John and I started this book. We agreed that on this first day he would try and create a quick, interesting but cheap meal – but that is all we planned. John just came along and looked in at the window and I started counting to fifteen . . .

Now, with our sprats and whiting, and this vague idea of contrast, we turned and made our way up the road, drifting through the rain while John pondered the possibilities in silence, and I hardly dared ask a question. What if it all went wrong? Where would lunch be then? I was hungry.

In the High Street, at the top of the pulse-racing hill which divides Lewes, we passed a big greengrocer's and John glanced in and said, "Leeks." We stopped and bought two, and after a pause, chose a very small fennel as well.

Off we went again, John now striding with more purpose in his step, as if some decision had been made – so I asked what it was all about, why the leeks and fennel, and he smiled and said, "It's partly for the contrast in colour – a nice sharp

green to go with the fish. Just because it's a simple, cheap meal, it doesn't mean it can't look good as well . . ."

He hesitated, and then the other truth came out. "Also, I'm a little worried about how the sprats might look when I've cooked them. They're small things and won't stand much heavy treatment. The green of the leek might help cover that up."

Now here was the tiny brick lane leading from the High Street to his restaurant. After a round trip of a mile and a half through dripping streets – but a total shopping time of less than four minutes – we had accumulated all the ingredients John needed in order to make a new meal, or most of them anyway: flavourings like seasalt and garlic were already in stock back at the kitchen.

Arriving at Kenwards, we pushed open the dark green front door and climbed the bare wooden stairs to the kitchen. The building itself is part-seventeenth century but the kitchen has elements of time-warp about it: exposed beams contrasting with gleaming white refrigerators; fresh herbs in pots at the side, but here in the centre a massive stainless steel table – on which John dumped his shopping and prepared to start work. At the back, a large gas-range waited to flicker into life; here were knives in racks, their blades regimented like bayonets; here were preparation boards, dark, wooden and well-used.

BASIC PREPARATION

John was rummaging in the vegetable rack, digging things out when he guessed they might be useful: a clove of garlic, half a battered lemon, a small onion, some potatoes.

Speaking as he worked, he said, "I'll use some of the leeks in a sauce for the whiting . . . and then I'll toss some in with the sprats to make a fishy salad. I suppose it'll be messy to eat but that's something you can accept at home."

I thought about the shouts in my house when the children spilled yoghurt on the tablecloth, but said nothing.

A word, though, about the fish. If you have

never cooked them, sprats are wonderful, oily little creatures; three to four inches long and so incredibly cheap that fishmongers tend to throw huge piles of them on the display where they lie like bright silver mountains. They have a rich taste, and you will find them in the colder months, such as on wet autumn days . . .

Whiting is a far more understated fish: between ten and twelve inches long it has a gentle mottled mushroom colour, a taste milder than cod, a texture softer than plaice. Some decry it as bland; that is going too far, but I was still curious to see what John would make of it.

He was meanwhile washing potatoes, not peeling them, but cutting them into chunks which were then put into a pot to boil.

Now, he skinned a small onion, cutting it into smallish pieces which were added to half a pint of water in a saucepan. This, he said, was the stock base – an important part of much of his fish cookery.

Moving quickly, he trimmed the ugly brown end pieces from the tops and bottoms of the two leeks and from the fennel, and put these in the stock too, together with three twists of ground black pepper and half a sliced and crushed garlic clove. Positively no salt though: "Add salt later," said John, "after you've found out whether it needs it or not. See what comes out of the other ingredients before deciding."

A point to note here is that nothing has been thrown away, except the onion skins. This kind of economy is another recurring theme, not in John's case because it saves money, but because it makes sense to get all the taste possible from what you buy. Of course, the fish bones were also destined to be used in the stock, which John set to boil and simmer. But it is at this point that some people might begin to feel uneasy.

Public attitudes to handling fish are not terribly robust. That is an understatement I picked up while standing behind the fish shop counter watching customers writhe in horror as I plunged my hands willy-nilly into salmon guts or

herring gills. The full truth is most people are scared stiff of touching fish, and I have no idea why this should be so: we are an island race, after all, and fishing is as much a part of our history as the Wars of the Roses and *Coronation Street*.

The over-riding shame of it is that developing skills with a knife, and facing the reality of food in the shape of bones, guts and eyes should really be a central part of our understanding and appreciation of what we eat. And besides all that, the skills themselves are really quite easy to pick up.

John was reaching for a whiting, saying, "Right, I'm going to fillet this . . ."

The method he used will work on any similarly shaped round fish – like cod, haddock, even trout and herring if you are careful with the finer bones.

Filleting whiting: the first cut

Firstly, he laid the fish on its side, pressing down firmly with his left hand while making a positive though not rough stroke with the knife along the backbone. The blade kept tight to the bone, retracing cuts where the flesh was missed or where the angle threatened to veer off into the body of the fillet.

Long, positive strokes traced the outline of the bones and ribs, arching out round the body cavity, peeling back the flesh until one complete side of the fish was free from bone, flapping out like a thick white flag.

Secondly, John folded this flesh back into place, turned the fish over so that the uncut side was now facing uppermost, and simply repeated the process.

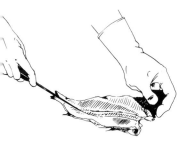

Filleting whiting: first fillet peeled away from bones

When this was finished he sliced the whole fillet into two halves (lengthways) and went on to the second whiting.

This took about forty seconds. It is not a very awesome task.

But as he worked, John was thinking about the direction of the meal forming under his hands. I was desperate to know what I was going to eat. John shrugged: "The ideas don't just come floating in as an ideal, perfect state," he said. "They are essentially based on the materials themselves, dictated by what is under your fingers. Contrast is

one idea to begin with, but even ways of achieving
that will vary from fish to fish. What I think about
is, what do *these ingredients* suggest or allow?"

Looking at the white blobs of fish waiting on
the stainless steel table, I did not think they
suggested very much. But John went on: "These,
I think I'll have to skin. It will look a bit nasty if I
leave the skins on and anyway they'll start to peel
when I begin cooking. Of course, the skins will
also add something to the stock, so what would
have been discarded on the plate will actually get
used."

Up came the blob of whiting – now down onto
the chopping board, held at the tail end while a
knife was pressed into the meat just near the
grasping fingers, angled both downwards and
along towards the other end of the fillet. While
gently sawing with the blade, John pulled at the
fish with one hand, drawing the whole length of it
back against the working knife. The meat came
away like unwrapping butter.

Of course, you can ask your fishmonger to do
this for you. But if you do have a go yourself and
find, perhaps, that the meat is not rising cleanly
from the skin, simply move the knife back a little
and go over it again a little more firmly.

John skinned all four fillets and then
announced, "It's crunch time." Decisions loomed.

Back to the leeks. These he now took and
began cutting – fine white and green slices fell in
sharp diagonals which frayed onto the wet brown
of the board. The trick of slicing at an angle
produced a better effect than simply cross-cut
rounds.

Now John divided these chopped leeks into
two camps: the green ovals, plus some chopped
fennel, went into a colander for cooking with the
sprats in a moment, while the white slices (less
pretty, but with a stronger flavour) and some
more fennel were mixed together for adding to the
stock a little later.

Only half the original small fennel was used, as
John had decided that more would swamp the
flavour of the dish.

What happened next was important both for this recipe and for many more which require a sauce base. The stock was strained and split into two: John poured half into a small frying pan, to which he also added a knob of butter and then set it on a low heat. The other half went into a saucepan which was put on a high gas to reduce by boiling.

Into that first frying pan with the stock and butter he placed the four whiting fillets, poaching them gently for only three to four minutes: "Never overcook fish," John warned. "It's too easy to ruin it."

While this was happening, and while the other half of the stock was still reducing madly, John turned his attention to the waiting sprats. He sprinkled a little seasalt over them then flung the fish into a butter-lined frying pan on a medium heat. They hissed and spat, and under the influence of a little prodding, began all too soon to look bruised – but no matter.

For now John added the green leek and fennel, mixing the ingredients with light tossing movements of a spatula, covering the tracks of cooking with bright green fronds of camouflage. After a total cooking time of about five minutes these were turned off and set briefly to warm, along with the whiting fillets.

And finally, John turned to the sauce, which by now had been reduced to a reasonable thickness.

Into this viscous liquid went the white cuts of leek and fennel, a squeeze from the battered lemon, and the drained fluid in which the whiting had been cooked. All this was left heating for just a moment or two longer while the plates were set out on the kitchen table. Then everything was served and we sat down to eat.

Thick-cut chunks of brown-skin potato; green and silver mix of sprats, leeks, fennel . . . whiting fillets circled by sauce. It was a lovely mix of contrasts and shared flavours. Leeks helped bridge the textural gap between sprats and whiting; the same stock base had been used for both cooking the fish and making the sauce; even

the poaching juice itself had been reused. It was a perfectly rounded meal, and it tasted wonderful.

And yes, I suppose it *was* a bit messy to eat. Sprats are bony little fish and eating them demands occasional pause to scrape bits from the lips and tongue; but when that threatened to become a bore we simply switched to the whiting fillet for a while. A contrast . . .

John munched away cheerfully. I asked what changes he might make to produce different meals from the same idea or similar ingredients and at once he began to talk about the possibilities. The ideas came little by little as the meal progressed, ended, and faded into the history of another day, another lunch.

VARIATIONS

John's view is that none of his dishes needs be taken simply as a blueprint for one meal. They are broad lines along which to travel while diving off here and there to add personal touches. As long as some basic rules are followed, he insists, there is no reason why someone could not take one idea and make something even better than the original. It is a philosophy which works particularly well with a flexible and forgiving food like fish.

So how might he change this first meal to produce a different taste?

His first point was that the strength of the sauce itself could be altered:

i Leave out the final addition of leek and fennel, said John, but add instead two teaspoons of Dijon mustard; more, if you like strong tastes.

ii For a sharper sauce, make it exactly as before, with a stock base, but add the pressing of half a lemon at the end, with or without the leek and fennel. A dessertspoon of white wine vinegar could replace the lemon juice for a slightly deeper flavour.

Beyond this, he suggested that a good way to cook the sprats alone would be to fry them for about three minutes in olive oil with some very finely sliced onion – making sure that the frying temperature did not rise too high or the onion would burn. Two or three very thin slices of fresh

ginger in the pan, he said, could make a slightly more interesting addition.

Whiting he did not see as bland at all: "It's subdued," said John, "but it is a pleasant fish and you could do quite a lot with it."

He proposed skinning the fillets, probing for any remaining bones, then cutting them into two-inch pieces and wrapping each in leaves of blanched spinach (see page 61-72), with a small piece of butter, a tiny corner of garlic and some pepper and salt in each parcel. Then bake them in a preheated medium oven for about ten minutes – or until each parcel is firm and tight to the touch: "Don't bother to be too meticulous about wrapping these," said John. "They'll tighten up and shrink as they cook."

An orange sauce based on a stock would be a beautiful accompaniment to such a meal. Make the stock as before, said John, then squeeze in half an orange when the liquid has thickened, and then reduce a little more. Dry vermouth and cream could also be added to this sauce.

The possibilities go on, but you may now like to remind yourself of what exactly happened for the meal we ate this time.

WHITING AND SPRATS WITH LEEK AND FENNEL
Ingredients for 4

2 × 12 oz (700 g) whole whiting

8-10 oz (225 -275 g) sprats

½ pint (275 ml) water

2 small leeks

1 small fennel

1 small onion

1 clove garlic

knob of butter

½ lemon

butter for frying sprats

seasalt, black pepper

1   Fillet and skin the whiting, and salt the sprats. Throw the whiting remains into a stock pan with about half a pint of water, three twists of pepper, leek and fennel trimmings (cut small), a chopped onion and half a chopped and crushed garlic clove. Simmer.

2   Slice the fennel and leek. Mix and make two piles – one of green, one of white.

3   Drain and split the stock after about fifteen minutes. Add a knob of butter to one part and in this poach the whiting for three to four minutes. Use the other part as a sauce base, reducing by boiling then finally adding white leek and fennel, a squeeze of lemon juice and the liquid from the poached whiting.

4   Fry the sprats in butter for two or three minutes, adding the green leek and fennel right at the end, shortly before serving.

2

Finnan Soup

Plaice and Salmon with Orange

Of all the days to go shopping for fish, Mondays are the worst, particularly for a restaurateur.

There is a reason for that, of course. Very often the only fish available in the shops at that end of the week is a left-over collection from Saturday, a slightly dull mix of limited range which irks the professional buyer.

Yet it seemed a fair test to put John Kenward through. For if a restaurateur cannot handle the panic of an awkwardly timed meal, who can?

To make the test a little sharper, I added the zest of importance: "Say it's a meal for someone you want to impress. Something worth sitting down for, you know? Say it really *matters . . .*"

These words were offered down the telephone; were received in silence. And later, on a street corner near the shops, hunched in a bitter wind that tore tears from the eyes, it was easier to understand John's failure to respond.

The enthusiasm of make-believe tends to fade when there are positive decisions to be made; when over-riding every thought is the fundamental realisation that somehow, Mondays and important

events are really best kept apart.

"If it's something special," said John ("gritted" is another way of putting it), "I'll want to make two courses . . ." We walked on to the fish shop, round-shouldered against the cold. "And because it's cold . . . some hot soup to start with would be a nice idea . . ."

My heart sank. Fish soup that is both edible and interesting has always seemed an impossible myth to me: myth rooted in mock turtle soup in poor restaurants where you played "hunt the lumpy bit" in liquid as clear as the shallow end of the civic baths.

What could possibly enliven a fish soup today?

Nothing interesting in the shop window, though we looked and looked – aware as much of absences as of the stock on sale. No mussels, no oysters, no succulent clams. A local boat had landed a Sunday catch and so there were some marvellous-looking whole plaice, plus a few left-over salmon tails, some whiting, a little cod fillet and flounders that were shamefully greying.

In all, it seemed a depressing array from which to trawl a meal that mattered. Yet I was missing one of the most important sections of a Monday fish shop.

"I'll include some smoked fish," said John. "It's an obvious choice when fish is short because it keeps better than the wet stuff."

Quite right, and a point I had no business overlooking in view of the fact that I have spent countless hours on my knees by the kiln at the back of my shop coaxing life into smoke-boxes under trays of waiting fillets.

For smoking is a preserving process involving chemical deposits on the surface of food. That's a fact I take comfort from as I have always found that getting a kiln to light involves going home smelling like November the Fifth. When I die, parts of me are going to carry on for ever.

John went into the shop and bought the following: one finnan haddock, one of those local plaice, and a rather tired-looking salmon tail which had to be wrenched from the talons of old age

(even the best of mongers try to encourage eternal life in fish by the use of ice and temperature control, but only so much is possible).

A finnan haddock, you may know, is a haddock smoked "on the bone". That is, a small whole fish with its head off, gutted and split and kiln-cured.

I asked John why he had chosen this bony kind of haddock instead of the fillets which were on sale and, toiling back up the hill towards the warmth of his restaurant kitchen, he replied, "The finnans looked good. Fillets might be easier to use but finnans give a slightly firmer, drier texture whereas the fillets tend to break up into flakes if you do anything with them."

And his other purchases?

He shrugged. "The plaice looked the best of the fresh fish, and I thought you might want to get rid of the salmon before it got much older . . ."

We returned to silence, each brooding on the meal ahead.

BASIC PREPARATION

Now safely installed behind his own preparation table, John explained that on this occasion he would use nothing but left-over weekend vegetables to make up the rest of this special lunch.

Whether that was arrogance or the simple calm of the truly skilled I don't know – but a quick glance at the vegetable rack disclosed only a few potatoes, a leek or two, some bits of celery and a little fruit . . . a range which mirrored the show down the road in the Monday fish shop. Not a great deal to inspire a cook.

"I'll use the smoked fish for the first course," John was saying, "and mix the plaice and salmon for the main meal. There's one plaice for two of us so I'll fillet it and divide the fillets between us. If the plaice had been much smaller I might have bought two and stuffed them with the salmon, but not at this size . . ."

(Note: restaurateurs tend to think in "portions". A home cook might very well stuff a larger plaice and make it do for two.)

John took up a knife. "Once I've filleted the plaice," he went on, "I can get a stock cooking and then make decisions about how to use the salmon. Also, I need to look at the plaice fillets and see what size they are and how firm they seem – all that will affect what I'm actually able to do with them. For instance, are they good enough to roll and hold their shape?"

We would see.

Filleting a plaice takes only moments, once you have grasped the basic idea. It is the fish created by God specifically to give amateur cooks something to practise on without getting too disheartened by failure – for it is difficult to ruin a plaice. The bone-structure of the beast springs no surprises. It is a flat frame with meat top and bottom and a small spiny hump where the backbone lies conveniently placed to indicate a good point to stick the knife in. To get the meat off this or any other flat fish, such as dabs, flounder, brill, there are two basic approaches.

The first is to "cross cut". That is, to take one whole fillet off the top of the fish and one off the bottom, in which case your only difficulty lies in urging the knife over the backbone without leaving vast and wasteful clumps of flesh behind. If you *do* fillet this way (and I prefer it) you would do best to chop the head off the plaice first, then face the thing towards you and poke the knife in just to the right of the backbone; slice away to the right until that half of the fillet comes free, then return to the middle and work your way over to the other side of the backbone with the blade of the knife, slicing and pulling the whole fillet away.

The other method, the one which John favours, is to "quarter cut", which gives two fillets from the top and two from the bottom. John did it this way:

Pressing the fish to the chopping-board he passed a knife along the backbone from head to tail, levering up the flesh to one side, pulling back a fold running the whole length of the fish. He sliced again and again to the bone, lifting flesh from the frame. When that "quarter" of the fish came

Quarter filleting a flat
fish: the first cuts

First quarter removed
from flat fish, second
fillet peeled back

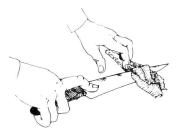

Skinning a quarter fillet
of flat fish, the knife
pressed firmly down
on to skin

free he returned to the backbone and sliced and peeled back the other part of the top fillet. Then he did the same on the underside.

Bones and head were chopped and added to half a pint of water in a saucepan, which he set to simmer. Then John skinned the fillets by imposing a knife between skin and flesh at the tail end and pulling the fish back across the working blade (see page 6).

Skins joined bones in the stock mix, together with one sliced onion, a crushed garlic clove, a little celery and some pepper.

To all those who find fillet skinning a pretty slippery business, I offer the following tip: use *two* knives – one to slice with, the other to jam point-in to the very tail of the fillet in order to hold the thing still. That way you don't leave a thumb's grasp of flesh hanging onto the end of the skin – a crime often spotted by fish shop customers who ask you to do the job for them and then wither you with a glance which shrieks "Waste!"

Interestingly, when John Kenward then filleted the salmon tail in the same way, and skinned it, he did *not* use the remains in the stock mix. "It's too oily and too dark," he said.

Now he washed and cut some skin-on potatoes which he set to boil. I asked what conclusions he had reached so far on the direction of the meal and he replied, "For the soup I have leeks and fresh ginger here which should mix well with the finnan haddock without any of the flavours being swamped.

"I used leeks in soup a few weeks ago and it worked well. And a point I'm bearing in mind is that I probably won't use much in the way of vegetables for the second course, except potatoes, so it makes sense nutritionally to use more with the starter."

"Why not simply use more vegetables in the second course?"

John smiled. "I suppose it's really because I don't want to be messing around with too many dishes."

Ah. Professional cooks do tend to generate a lot of washing-up when they work – probably because there's usually some other poor soul at the sink to do the skivvying. On this occasion at least, John was planning to limit the donkey work.

What plans, though, had he made for the main course?

"None." And he got on with the soup.

Actually, the first step John took in making the soup turned out later to be an error.

When he had washed and trimmed the leek (trimmings into the stock) he cut it diagonally, producing long slices which we subsequently found difficult to spoon into our mouths. Simple round cuts would have caused fewer splashes down the shirt front.

Next, he filleted the finnan haddock, which is a fairly difficult job for the inexperienced cook because the exposed bone structure of the average finnan resembles craggier portions of the Pennine Way. Running a knife over that sort of terrain without leaving clumps of meat behind takes some concentration – but do try it.

Firstly, hold the fish skin downwards, start with your knife on the central bone and slice out to one side, pushing hard into the rib-bones. Then do the same to the other side. Remember to haul the knife back a little and retrace the cut if you start to miss flesh; and make sure the slices are firm and positive.

The fillets you achieve this way *are* much better-textured than ordinary smoked haddock "off the bone", which is important in a soup when you want to avoid ending up eating mush.

John cut his fillets into pieces an inch long, but hung onto the meat-rich bones. These, together with the peelings of a small piece of fresh ginger, he put into a saucepan to which he then added half the strained stock mix and a little more water.

The other half of the stock went into a frying pan, after which John grated some of the peeled ginger onto the waiting slices of leek.

John explained what was happening:

"I don't want to bake the plaice and salmon," he said, lighting the gas under both portions of stock. "That's not for any particular cooking reason, just because I don't want to turn on a bloody great oven for so little fish. I think most people cooking at home would feel the same."

He went on, "I don't just want to produce a fillet of salmon and a fillet of plaice – I suppose I want to do something a bit more colourful, something that will be interesting and perhaps contain a small surprise . . ."

John now began moving as if all decisions had at last been made. Turning to the four slim fillets of salmon he sliced one tiny long fragment from each – which he then cut into fragments and laid at the head end of the four plaice fillets.

Here, he hesitated, eyes ranging the orderly kitchen shelves as if something had been left there and he couldn't remember what. Now he discovered a cluster of fruit on a shelf, amongst which a single orange shone out like a small Belisha beacon. John said, "Ah, an orange." (Honestly.)

He leapt upon this orange as if it was the missing piece of a jigsaw found under the sofa after an afternoon's search. Ingredients were dictating ideas, it was a classic example.

A rummage in the drawer produced a zester – a piece of equipment with tiny talons which looks like the sort of thing police arrest football yobs for carrying to matches.

Its job was to coax minute scrapings from the orange, but if you, like me, have no zester at home, scrape bits off the skin with a knife.

These scrapings now joined the salmon fragments at the end of the plaice fillets, together with a tiny sprinkling of salt and pepper.

"I'm going to roll these fillets now," said John, speaking as he worked. "The thing is to start with the thick end and roll towards the tail, because that leaves the thinner part of the fillet on the outside and helps make the shape.

"Also, you can see that the side I'm stuffing is what was the skin side, which doesn't look nice.

This way we have a smoother side on the outside of the roll.

"The advantage of rolling plaice anyway is that the fillets stay whole like that. If you just poach them they can break up. This way, the roll shrinks in on itself and becomes firm . . ."

In seconds, each quarter fillet had been eased into tiny but magnificent swiss roll-like shapes, ready for the pan.

But leaving them for a moment, John returned to the soup stock, which he strained once more, then tasted before adding salt, pepper and the juice of half a lemon.

A knob of butter went into the other, poaching stock, plus the juice of the zested orange.

"Now I'll reduce it slightly," said John, turning up the gas. "I want to get it to the state in which I would want to serve it . . ."

In eerie silence we watched the liquid seethe – all that moved in the kitchen.

Then John moved swiftly once more.

The leeks and sliced ginger were thrown into the soup mix, cooked for one minute and then were joined by the sliced finnan fillets.

"The timing is important now," said John. "I'll let the finnans cook for just one minute while the salmon and plaice go into the other pan, and by that time the soup will be ready to serve."

Be warned, the poaching pan was turned down very low before the rolled plaice and the salmon fillets were placed carefully into the liquid. Then John covered the frying pan and announced that the first course would be ready to eat.

We ate.

The soup was both fresh and warming, if that is possible to accept. Outside, the bitter wind buffeted the vast kitchen skylight. Inside, we drank the flavours of warm ginger and smoky fish. And yes, the leeks dropped off the spoon but otherwise, in all ways, God was in his Heaven.

And the main course was wonderful precisely because of that chance addition of orange which gave a freshness to the oily salmon and removed

all danger of blandness from the plaice. It was indeed the perfect example of why experimenting in the kitchen – letting chance have its turn at the pot – is worthwhile. Because it worked.

I should add that John did not simply plonk the salmon and plaice fillets on to our plates, but arranged them into some balanced shape. Yet he specifically refused to devote too much time to this purely visual aspect of cookery – he has strong views on cooking up a picture, believing that food *should* look good but that "style" should never get in the way of content or flavour.

But of course, the meal that has just gone seldom excites a chef, and John was already discussing alternative ways of using the same ingredients . . .

Consider these possibilities:

VARIATIONS

THE SOUP: John proposed creaming the same basic soup, adding a little potato to thicken the mix, then liquidising the lot and adding fresh cream at the end, just before reheating.

The result would have been a far heavier, more filling dish which could even make a quick, satisfying lunch.

"Or if you want to be really flash you could use slivers of smoked salmon," said John. "Or just the tail-end bits of smoked salmon which go as sandwich pieces. Use those instead of finnan haddock."

A third idea was to turn the whole dish into a pasta meal, cooking sheaves of green pasta in the fish stock: thus adding the thickening effect which pasta has. Again, finnans or smoked salmon would be added right at the end.

And for those who want to make this dish in isolation, without an existing fish stock to draw upon, John recommended making a basic stock of garlic, lemon, onion and water.

THE MAIN MEAL: Here, John returned to the idea of using the plaice unfilleted.

"I could have stuffed the fish with finnan fillets and leek," he said, "cooking the stuffing a little

first with some butter, then chopping it finely.

"I would have sliced open the back of the plaice, pushed in the leek and haddock and baked it for fifteen minutes – not covering it, baking rather than steaming, because it looks better cooked that way."

I suggested that mussels might have been used instead of salmon as a cheaper way of adding colour and texture to the meal, and John agreed that it should work well.

"Use some mussels to stuff the fillets and a few more to poach with the sauce," he said.

"You would have to boil the mussels for a couple of minutes in a little water, keeping the liquid for the sauce. Then you could liquidise some of them for the stuffing with some pepper and lemon – and *fold* the plaice fillets over, rather than roll, because the mussel mix might spread under pressure . . ."

Here, though, are the details of the meal we actually ate that day:

FINNAN SOUP
Ingredients for 2

1 medium finnan haddock
a little celery or other vegetable to add to a stock
1 medium onion
1 garlic clove
a little fresh ginger
1 leek
seasalt, black pepper
½ lemon

1 Fillet the finnan, cutting the pieces into one-inch lengths, adding the bones to a basic stock mix together with peelings from the ginger, and the leek trimmings.

2 Simmer the stock for some minutes, then strain and add salt, pepper, lemon juice to taste.

3   Cut the leek into rounds, add this plus a little grated ginger to the stock mix and cook for one minute.

4   Add the finnan fillets and cook for a further minute.

PLAICE AND SALMON WITH ORANGE
Ingredients for 2

1 whole plaice (1 lb, 450 g)
8 oz (225 g) salmon fillet
vegetables for stock:
1 onion
a little celery
1 garlic clove
1 orange
knob of butter
black pepper

1   Fillet and skin the plaice, using bones to make fish stock (together with water, chopped onion, crushed garlic clove, a little chopped celery and some pepper).

2   Fillet and skin the salmon tail but discard bones and skin.

3   Cut fine strips from the salmon fillets, and place these at the top of the plaice fillets at the "head" end. Add a little of the zest of one orange and roll down to the tail.

4   Add the juice from the orange, plus a knob of butter, to the stock, then reduce by boiling.

5   Place the stuffed fillets and separate salmon fillets in the simmering stock, cover and cook at a very low heat for up to ten minutes.

6   Arrange the pieces on a plate and add the stock sauce.

3

SQUID SOUP

MUSSELS WITH FENNEL

LEMON SOLE WITH WATERCRESS SAUCE

SCALLOPS WITH SPRING ONION

A lump of old chicory hit the bin with a thump. "That can go," said John, "it's served its time in there . . ." He went on rummaging through the vegetables now murmuring that he wanted some fennel but he was sure he had a bit somewhere, didn't he?

Yes, or a little, anyway. The remains of a small fennel were taken out at last and placed on the stainless steel table with the rest of the ingredients, which seemed to stretch for ever across the kitchen. We had decided on a meal for just four people, yet there seemed so much to do, so much to work on. Had we overshot this time?

The whole trouble with the kind of meal outlined here is that at first glance it does seem an imposing task, complex enough to turn even the strongest of cooks into Little Willy Wetlegs. For who, by choice, would design a lunch for friends involving four apparently demanding dishes all to be served simultaneously?

Yet the truth is that you need not skip this chapter for an easier one. Really. Taken either as individual meals or – more properly – a massed collection, the four dishes John cooked on this day were almost as easy as oven-ready chips. Please do keep that in mind as the pages turn and the ideas unfold.

The detailed brief was to produce something interesting for a group of friends rather than mere guests: that is, the sort of people who will not judge you by the Marmite streak in your butter dish and from whom you do not wish to cower in the kitchen.

As John Kenward said, staggering from the fish shop with a lovely mix of food, "This really has got to be very easily presented. I might even make it cold because I'm supposed to be with friends and so I don't want to spend a lot of time cooking . . ."

What he actually bought – chosen from seventeen varieties on sale that day – was four scallops, two small lemon soles, two pounds of live mussels, two very small squid and four herrings. Forget the herrings, though. As John admitted at the time, "I don't know why I bought them really. I never cook the bloody things." And as it turned out he did not cook these ones either. They were left in the fridge, a mouldering monument to impulse buying.

So the final useful array of produce lined up there included all the above fish (except the herrings) together with two onions, a bunch of watercress, some garlic, four carrots, four large spring onions, half a lemon, a small dish of thick cream, a bit of fennel and a really awful looking end of old celery.

"I'm going to cook . . . erm . . ." John

stopped and fell silent. A Black Hole of indecision swirled briefly round the kitchen. "No," he went on suddenly, "I'm going to do the sort of meal that will make people mix and talk. Not a single dish. More variety – and cold, so people can sit round a table and pick. And it won't matter if some of the dishes are a bit messy because it's friends . . ."

What followed was an enormously successful meal which took just thirty-five minutes to prepare as one complete task – though here, I have broken it down into sections for easier understanding. You will see that the fish stock was used mostly for the squid soup, but splashes were used in the other three dishes as well. You will probably want to vary the type and amount of stock you make if preparing the dishes separately.

BASIC PREPARATION

John started with the mussels.

Firstly, he discarded those that were broken or dead. How do you tell? If it is broken, throw it away; if it is *open,* tap the shell or squeeze it up and down a few times, and if it then gently closes it is alive and ready to die for you. If no amount of tapping produces movement, throw the creature away.

I received many after-hours calls at my fish shop from customers wanting to be guided through this test. Normally, callers would begin truculently – "Those damned mussels you sold me are all open . . ." I would ask them to bang the bag containing the mussels and there would be a muffled clonk, followed by, "Good heavens . . ." On these nights I would go home and be rude to my wife.

John now briefly washed and "bearded" the mussels, pulling away any remaining threads visible on the seams, before setting the pile to one side while he filleted the lemon soles: "I'll have to, because they're to be shared by four of us."

He "quarter cut" the two fish, sliding the knife up the middle of the backbone and paring the flesh away to each side, as described on page 14.

In fact, filleting did not go exactly as planned this time, because the brittle bones near the tail of

Opening a scallop, knife inserted, thumb wedging shells apart

Cutting meat away from flat shell of scallop

Scallop meat has been cut away from flat shell; skirt is scraped off shell

Cutting and removing meat from round shell of scallop

one fish snapped under the knife and stuck to the flesh. John swore and then painstakingly sliced these bones from the fillet before carrying on with the task. (An alternative method when this happens is to finish the filleting, then spread the meat out and remove all left-over bones at the end. Either method is boring).

That over with, John now skinned all eight resulting fillets (see page 15) throwing the skins, bones and pink slimy fish roes into a stock pot with two pints of water and two small, chopped onions. With this set to boil, he turned to the scallops.

The trouble with opening scallops is that they act a little like giant clams – those things you will have seen on the movies, trapping divers by the foot. While scallops are not up to this sort of drama they certainly resent you poking things inside their shells.

Hence their reluctance to let you stick a knife in the slit where the two shell halves meet. Keep trying. When you have succeeded, and have woggled your knife a little to make a decent parting of the shells they will still try and close on you. All you do then is put your thumb into the slit while making a better cut with the knife. As John did, you must aim to insinuate the blade between the meat and the flat part of the shell, and when you have succeeded, the scallop springs open, leaving you to scoop out the meat from the top and plop it onto the table.

John was lucky because his scallops were a little old and were therefore gaping when he started work on them. The really freshest examples will not only resist but will throb pitifully for a few seconds when you have scooped them from the shell, thus tinging your victory with sadness.

John now had to clean his scallops – something he did speedily but with care, using a very sharp knife to separate the surrounding skirt of useless brown gristle from the white flesh and brilliant, edible orange coral. He then pared away the dull white pad of hard material which is situated roughly opposite this coral and which looks

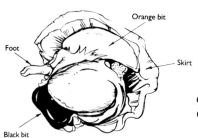

Orange bit

Foot

Skirt

Black bit

Scallop meat
before cleaning and trimming

Scallop meat ready for cooking

COOKING THE SCALLOPS

almost the same as the central body – but not quite.

Finally, he cut of the "foot": the small appendage less than a centimetre long which sticks out from the main body of the scallop and which (we think) links the top and bottom of the shell.

It all sounds very complicated, I know, but the skill is quickly learnt, and you could always ask your fishmonger to give a demonstration or to do it for you.

Now John began to fine down his ideas.

"I'll use the stock mainly as a basis for the squid soup," he said. "And because these squid are so small I'll try boiling them whole in the stock instead of cleaning them first. It's something I've never tried before but it's probably worth it – there's less work that way and the ink and juices don't get wasted if we cook them whole."

In went the squid and with this move the meal began to take a proper shape.

The two tiny fish remained cooking for about ten minutes while John turned to the scallops.

"These with spring onions would almost certainly be good," he said. "I've used them together before and I know it produces a good blend of colour, texture and shape – whereas watercress and scallops wouldn't work, not visually – they'd just be a heap if you cooked them."

So he reached for a knife and began trimming the huge spring onions (so beefy they looked as spring-like as a pair of wellingtons), throwing the tops and bottoms into the stock, murmuring, "These will be fried quickly with the scallops . . . where's the butter . . .?"

Butter was found – John always uses the unsalted kind – and a spoonful thrust into a small but thick frying pan, which John set on a low heat while he cut a few tiny rings from the white ends of each spring onion. He used that wonderful, endless rocking motion with the knife – so fast you expect to see bits of finger joining the veg, but

never do. Using only half an inch from each onion, John tossed a few of the rings into the buttered pan and kept the rest back for later, leaving the gas low enough to allow onion and butter to merge gently.

Now he sliced the scallops horizontally into three before moving to the spring onions once more, cutting them lengthways into fine green and white strips. Why? "Because they will look better in the dish that way, and they'll cook quicker and won't lose their colour."

Now came a period of frantic activity.

Up went the gas under the frying pan. John explained, "I want the scallops to fry, not poach, so the pan must be hot. To get that wonderful flavour and smell, frying is actually very important – if you poach them they are good, but they don't develop the same potency of flavour. And I'm not adding any stock to the pan – I'll just fry them in butter so that the scallops almost catch . . ."

The pan itself, he stressed, had to be thick to let the process work properly. Thin pans would cool with the contact of the fish.

In went the scallops, hissing fiercely as they touched the fat, soon moved on by a prodding wooden spoon as John continued, "If they cool on contact you have lost it. I'm sealing the flavour in with real heat . . . now I'm reducing the heat . . . they've had about a minute. Now I'll cook them more gently for a minute or so more . . ." He squeezed in a few drops of lemon juice and when the scallops had been cooking for a total time of just over two minutes he flung in the spring onion shafts.

The smell now filling the kitchen was of the kind that makes adults dribble and children ask for a bag of crisps. It was marvellous: a rich waft of butter, hot onion and fresh seafood; a smell you felt in your clothes and hair but didn't care about because cooking should be composed of such sensations.

Another squeeze of lemon juice went into the pan with just two dessertspoonfuls of stock. "Only a small amount of stock because I don't want the

onions to go soggy," John explained. "I want them to fry rather than steam – but I've put that little bit in because it's tending to catch . . ."

After a further two minutes of cooking – that is, a total time of about four minutes – John prodded the food onto a plate, leaving butter and juice in the pan, which he now returned to a high gas, adding a few more spoonfuls of stock and a shake of pepper.

Working quickly with a spoon he scraped away the tasty brown ring marks which the sauce had created at the sides and bottom of the pan, mixing it with the liquid to give flavour and colour.

The sauce was allowed to reduce slightly in the heat, then was poured over the waiting scallops and onions.

It could have been eaten right then, hot – or left to cool as John had planned. He was already moving on.

COOKING THE LEMON SOLE

This part would need a finished stock to poach the fillets in, so John first saw to that part of the process.

Out of the boiling stock came the two squid (you remember, they were cooking whole) which John quickly decapitated, revealing the ends of the transparent backbones. If you have never seen squid backbones before you will be in for a surprise here: they look like long, thin pieces of cellophane – like something lobbed from a channel ferry to lodge uncomfortably down the creature's neck. Not so. They are meant to be there, and to get them out you can pinch the top end with a knife jammed against the chopping-board, then gently withdraw the main body of the fish. The bone stays where it is. (A detailed explanation appears on page 97).

That done, John cut the squid into thin rings, pushing out their insides with a thumb and throwing the resulting mess into the stock pot, which continued to bubble on a low gas.

The rings themselves, John put by for using when the stock was ready to become soup.

In a fresh burst of action the tops of the

watercress clumps were pulled off to eat raw later, while the bigger, lower leaves were chopped up for cooking soon. The stalks were cut and put into the stock together with the chopped stump of old celery.

Finely sliced watercress was added to each lemon sole fillet, plus a small knob of butter, then each fillet was folded over in half, ready to cook.

To do this, John added a little more butter to the same frying pan he had used for the scallops; a splash more stock joined it, and the lemon fillets were gently laid to rest there, and covered. The gas was left very low.

Christine, one of John's helpers, drifted into the kitchen at this stage and began idly helping herself to the cooling scallops. "That's how I saw it being eaten," said John. "Everybody picking."

About five minutes later, when the lemon sole fillets were firm and only just out of the translucent stage, they were taken from the pan and arranged quickly on a plate, separated by sprigs of raw watercress. Then the chopped watercress was tossed into the frying pan with some more butter, and gently stewed with a splash more stock for about one minute. This sauce was then poured over the fish. Another dish completed.

SOUP . . . AND MUSSELS

Before the lemon sole fillets were even cooked, John had begun work on the final stage of the meal. And at this point he was poised to bump into a lovely piece of culinary inspiration.

After sieving the stock to clear out the worst of the debris John was pausing over the remaining clear liquid, watching it bubble on the gas.

He suddenly said, "We've got this hot stock, and I need to cook the mussels – let's boil them in this . . ."

Whoosh. In went the mussels, on went the lid, up went the gas. It was done before you could say suck-it-and-see, and we gathered in curiosity round the steaming pot as John explained, "Normally I'd boil up some water separately and

cook the mussels in that – maybe add some pepper, garlic and perhaps a little wine. But it occurs to me that doing it this way we'll have that wonderful salty flavour of the mussels as a base for the soup."

Three minutes later the mussels were open and orange but still puffy and light. Then a small amount of finely chopped fennel was thrown in, and seconds later the whole lot was dredged back out with a perforated spoon, piled into a bowl and left to cool. (If you cannot bear the suspense, let me tell you now that the mussel idea was brilliant: it worked wonders on the soup. Now read on.)

John next strained the stock through muslin, threw away the bits, and returned the thick, fragrant liquid to the saucepan, adding two fluid ounces of thick cream and the rest of those tiny spring onion rounds he had cut up earlier. This was left to simmer for just a minute or two.

At this point I asked John why he had ignored the carrots which were still spread out on the table like the fingers of a thumbless hand. He gave a "Yes, yes all right" sort of glance and swiftly but silently cut two of the things into fine slivers, which went into the soup, together with two chopped cloves of garlic – and the squid rings.

A minute later it was done and served. That was it. Four dishes surrounding a basket of home-made bread in the centre of the kitchen table: warm soup, mussels with fennel, scallops with spring onions, lemon sole with watercress sauce.

We began to eat.

My own favourite was probably the sole, because the watercress itself still had the firm, barely cooked freshness which perfectly suited the gently poached fish.

The scallops made a wonderful counterpoint of rich solidity, and the mussels – which we pulled by hand from the shell, picking at pieces of fennel as we found them – were a diverting side dish.

As for that soup, the mussel juice really had added a depth which, combined with the cream, produced an effect approaching that of salty cheese. Even the carrot added bite. It was a great

dish.

We finished, settled, and began talking about other ideas.

VARIATIONS

THE SOUP: An obvious alternative for this dish would have been to have made it into a full meal by itself, by using the scallops and leaving in the mussels. John said, "I would have fried the scallops in the same way but then, instead of using a little butter and a tiny amount of stock, I would have added all the stock and whatever was with it."

His view was that, with or without the additional ingredients, some added fresh ginger could have altered the soup – perhaps to a winter dish. Another point is that if soup had been taken off this menu only small amounts of stock would have been needed – leaving some to be frozen for future use, which can be helpful when you don't feel like boiling up fish bones.

MUSSELS: "Stuffed mussels would have been lovely," said John. "And it would make it seem a much more expensive meal. You could cook the mussels in boiling water, then take them out of the shell and mix together some butter, parsley, cayenne pepper, garlic – and some white wine or vermouth. Then you take each shell and put the meat back in and splodge in your mixture . . ."

And then serve?

"Not necessarily. You could keep them for a day or two in the fridge if you had to, then just put them in a hot oven for ten minutes before eating – though it would really be a starter . . ."

LEMON SOLE: Here, John proposed dealing with them almost as whole fish – but this, of course, would mean one fish for each person.

"I could have trimmed their sides (with scissors) and removed some of the tail so that it didn't make too much of a mess when it was cooked. Then I would have cut open the backbone on two sides, leaving flaps. I'd have taken mussels out of their shell and some of the watercress and

chopped them up together with some butter and pushed the mixture into the fish cavity, folded the flaps back over and baked it for fifteen minutes. No sauce – just butter flowing out of it . . . beautiful . . ."

And another way of dealing with the scallops?

John shrugged. The scallops, he pointed out, had already gone into the soup. He was tired of this meal. For him, it was already time to be thinking of other things. He pushed back his chair, got up, and started clearing plates.

For you, I detail below the things John did on this occasion to make the whole meal. But I have divided the dishes, in case you would like to try them one at a time.

SQUID SOUP
Ingredients for 4

For the stock

flat fish bones

2 onions

4 large spring onions (trimmings only)

watercress stalks

2 celery stalks

2 pints (1 litre 140 ml) water

1 lb (450 g) squid

½ lb (225 g) mussels, if desired

¼ small fennel (if cooking the mussels for the
    next dish)

2 fl oz (55 ml) thick cream

spring onions, sliced rounds

2 small carrots

2 garlic cloves

1   Boil your stock ingredients in about two pints of water, adding the whole squid and letting them cook for about ten minutes.

2   Remove squid, cut into rings and keep these. Push the guts out with your fingers and throw them back into the soup.

3   After two or three more minutes, sieve the liquid and return to the gas – boil vigorously and throw in the mussels if desired. Also add some chopped fennel if required for the separate mussel dish.

4   After four or five minutes dredge out the mussels and fennel and add two ounces of thick cream while still simmering.

5   Add sliced rounds of spring onion, some fine slivers of two carrots, two chopped and crushed garlic cloves – and the squid rings. Mix for one minute, then serve with or without the mussels.

MUSSELS WITH FENNEL
Ingredients for 4 as a starter

(Allow I lb (450 g) mussels per person for a full meal with salad & bread)

2 pints (I litre I40 ml) fish stock (see **SQUID SOUP**) or you can use pepper, garlic, wine and chopped onions

2 lb (900 g) live mussels

¼ small fennel

1   Boil the stock ingredients for ten to fifteen minutes. Throw in the live, cleaned mussels and cover the pan.

2   Chop a small quantity of fennel and throw this in when the mussels have been cooking for three minutes and are almost ready.

3   One minute later, dredge out the mussels and serve. Don't forget to include the fennel when serving.

4   The remaining stock can be used as a soup base, or frozen, or thrown away.

LEMON SOLE WITH WATERCRESS SAUCE

Ingredients for 4 as a starter

(Allow one fish per person as a main meal)

2 × 12 oz (700 g) lemon soles

small bunch watercress

butter, knob

fish stock (see **SQUID SOUP**)

1   Fillet and skin the lemon soles, cutting so that there are four fillets per fish. (Use the bones and skin to help the stock).

2   Add a little finely chopped watercress to each fillet, plus a small knob of butter, then fold each fillet in half.

3   Warm some butter in a frying pan, and add to this a very small amount of stock. Keep the gas low.

4   Add the lemon sole fillets, and cover the pan.

5   Test them for firmness five minutes later. If cooked, remove from the pan and arrange on plates with sprigs of fresh watercress.

6   Add more chopped watercress to frying pan plus more butter and a few more spoonfuls of stock. Cook for about one minute.

7   Serve with the lemon sole fillets.

SCALLOPS WITH SPRING ONION

Ingredients for 4 as a starter

(Allow 3 scallops per person for a main meal)

8 scallops

8 spring onions

butter

juice of ½ lemon

fish stock (see **SQUID SOUP**)

1   Open and clean the scallops. Trim the spring onions (trimmings in the stock) and slice lengthways two or three times. If your scallops are large, cut them horizontally into two or three.

2   Heat a knob of butter in a thick frying pan and throw in a few slivers or rounds of onion to give it flavour.

3   Turn heat up high and when pan is very hot, throw in the sliced scallops, tossing them regularly with wooden spoon.

4   After a minute, squeeze in a little lemon juice, still prodding with spoon, then cook for a further minute.

5   Add the sliced spring onions and more lemon juice. Also, about two dessertspoonfuls of fish stock. Keep prodding.

6   After a further two minutes remove scallops and onions from pan, add a few more spoonfuls of stock to pan plus shake of pepper. Scrape and stir and mix the liquid for one minute, then pour over scallop meat and serve.

4

LOBSTER TERRINE WITH LOBSTER SAUCE

Standing in the fish shop I stared at the lobster which John was holding and sympathised with its obvious loss. Somewhere along the line it had shed a leg; I, on the other hand, was without a fish business.

By the time this stage of our book was reached I had sold up – bowed out in order to write. This was my first return, and it was an odd moment.

Disposing of a business you have started and watched grow is rather like shooting the family dog: emotional. You have lost something but retain an odd sensation of wanting to touch the place where it was.

It was no longer *my* fish that John pondered as we discussed the forthcoming meal – it was someone else's. And just as good but different, affecting perhaps my perception of this meal and others that followed. Who knows? Perhaps I sympathised later with Hopalong Lobster as we settled down together at the same table and, gently, I ate him.

This day was overcast. But for once it was not a factor we needed to consider when discussing the meal, because John and I had decided on a change for this shopping trip. He was to prepare a

special fish starter for a lot of guests – up to ten – and because it was so out of the ordinary he was doing the work in advance.

In other words, this marvellous dish has the added advantage that you can prepare it two or even three days before your guests arrive, leaving you to give your attention to the main course on the day itself.

Hefting the cooked lobster, John pointed out that, legless or not, it was heavy: a sign of a good, full body of meat.

"I'll use lobster because the meal will be important," he said, "but I could make a good terrine from so many other things here – mussel meat, crab, smoked fish, smoked salmon . . ."

Wasn't he worried about using a lobster he had not killed and cooked himself? John shook his head. "Not if it's going to be used straight away," he said. "But anyway I'm going to process this into a terrine so it doesn't have to have a perfect texture: in fact, it's an ideal way of using a lobster which isn't so fresh as it might be."

Glancing back round the shop his eyes fell on a huge, bright plaice which was quite obviously local: its spots shone with colour, and when we moved across for a surreptitious test its flesh was firm and springy.

"It's nice," John conceded. "I'll use this as the basis for the dish." So we bought it.

That plaice, by the way, weighed almost two pounds and later yielded about fourteen ounces in skinned fillets. The lobster weighed only twelve ounces at the start but gave us more than five ounces of picked meat. I offer these weights now so that you can appreciate the impressive ratio of fish input to people fed: that is, about a pound and a quarter of fish provided a starter for about ten people. This may help you work out your own shopping needs when cooking for fewer or more guests.

As it happened, we had to buy nothing else to go into this terrine because John knew that everything we would need was already back in the restaurant. So up the hill we trudged, playing the

usual Lewes game of compressed conversations –
words squeezed between panted breaths,
adjectives and subjects chosen for brevity rather
than interest.

Then there was the restaurant and the smell
of coffee warming; lobster and plaice on the table.
A pause before John began to work.

Although on this occasion we had deliberately
cut the uncertainty of the direction John would
take – we knew it would be a terrine – there were
still decisions to be made, and experiments to play
with. In fact, as we discuss later, terrines have so
many possibilities they are really exciting to make;
you can put your personal stamp on them with the
smallest piece of invention.

BASIC PREPARATION

John began by filleting the huge plaice, quarter-
cutting the beast (paring down the backbone as
shown on pages 14 and 15). He explained, "I'm
starting with this because the plaice will be used as
the base – and because I want to make a stock, so
I'll get that on right away."

Four thick, juicy fillets came off the bones, and
the fish frame was quickly chopped in three or four
places then put into a large pot with two pints of
water. The fish skin was "peeled" from the fillets
with a very sharp knife and thrown into the stock.
One small onion, some stalks of parsley and a very
few pieces of left-over celery and fennel were also
chopped, together with just half a clove of garlic,
and added to the water mix.

The celery and fennel, of course, just
happened to be the left-overs available in the
vegetable rack; they added their own taste, but
other remnants would have done just as well.

Two other points should be mentioned here.
The first is that – as always – John put a great deal
of care into chopping these stock vegetables,
reducing everything to really small fragments.

The reason, as he explained, was that "you
can extract the maximum flavour in the shortest
time if you cut small." A detail only, but then
effective cookery relies on this sort of ground
rule, out of which those extra degrees of taste are

squeezed onto the tongue.

The second point is that, for the first time in this series of dishes, John kept back the brown skin from the onion instead of throwing it away. I asked why, and he explained, "The skins are for the lobster sauce which I'm going to make later. They'll add colour and a little bitterness. I don't normally use onion skins for fish stock because usually I'm making sauces which are going to be pale, but with crustacea more colour comes out in the cooking so I'm not worried about putting more colour in."

The whole theme of colour recurs time and again in Kenward cookery – sometimes, as on this occasion, it is a significant creative spark for a particular meal; not to say that the whole dish will be subjugated by the desire for a particular colour, but that colour itself can act as an impetus, an initial thought.

John explained, "What's happening now is a good example – I have one ingredient, in this case the lobster, and because I know it will create a redness in the dish I look for something green as a contrast. Very corny, but there . . . So I know I've got some parsley and I'll use that in the dish; as much as anything for its colour."

So colour was not the truly original inspiration for this dish – the choice of lobster was that – and yet it formed a significant part of the basic decision-making process after one step had been taken.

As John pointed out, the spark for a meal can come from one of a number of general areas, including texture, nutrition, and, of course, taste itself. "Many people only consider taste as the spark, which is a pity," said John. "Texture, for instance, is a very interesting part of a meal."

But now, pausing only to twist four or five small showers of black pepper into the stock ("Black because it has more flavour and aroma") John was ready to attack the lobster.

As far as I was concerned, the lobster we addressed that day possessed one huge

advantage: it was dead. Many cookery books will
instruct you only to buy live lobster, and to go
through the process of killing it yourself. That's all
very well, and a very fresh dish will certainly
emerge from the gruesome tussle if you do so.
But I have never found it possible to kill one of the
creatures without a certain fairly sharp twinge of
regret.

What they tend not to tell you in the books is
that really fresh lobsters fight like mad when they
catch the whiff of boiling, salted water which is to
be their final taste of a strangely unkind
environment. Not that they can hurt you, because
some thoughtful fisherman will have tied their
claws; but to watch the body and tail flapping in
wild distress, to feel the battle for survival going
on under your hand as you approach the pot . . .
well, these things leave their mark.

Not that everyone suffers the same
hesitation. Younger staff at my Lewes shop
positively looked forward to despatching live
shellfish. They would give the creatures
alliterative names like Larry Lobster and Kevin
Crab. Then, volunteering for the job of
executioner, they would carry Kev or Larry
towards the steaming pot for a final baptism with
the muttered invitation, "Time for a hot bath . . ."

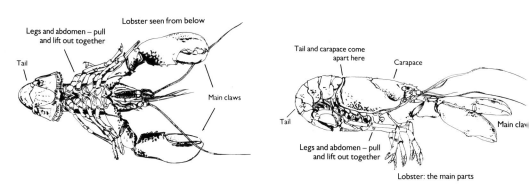

Lobster seen from below

Legs and abdomen – pull
and lift out together

Tail

Main claws

Tail and carapace come
apart here

Carapace

Tail

Main claw

Legs and abdomen – pull
and lift out together

Lobster: the main parts

If you ever have to do it, my advice is to get the water as boiling hot as your stove can manage, and then get it over with quickly – head first for Larry, don't just singe his tail. About ten minutes later (for a one pound or so fish) he will be transformed into something very tasty and anonymous.

John faced no such problem on this day; his job was just to get the meat from the beast.

How do you do that?

John did it this way: first he pulled the lobster into three basic parts – the major claw(s), the head section, and the tail. Then, using a sharp knife, he cut the tail lengthways in half, cutting the soft white shell underneath, not on top. The meat came out as two thin slices with a little mess at the end which had to be washed off. He finely cut most of each slice but kept back a little to be chunked up later.

A main claw of a lobster: separating the parts with a cloth

Next, he pulled the claw joints apart, protecting his hands from the sharp edges by using a cloth. Then he cracked the main joints using the flat of a heavy-bladed knife (a hammer will do, but be careful: lobster shells vary enormously in strength, and a misjudged blow will have you picking lobster meat off the walls).

Now he flicked the revealed joint and claw meat into a dish: "I'm not being meticulous with this because none of this will be wasted anyway . . ." This becomes clearer later.

With a final heave, John then pulled the leg section away from the head shell or carapace. This leg section he split very carefully with a knife and scraped into the dish, muttering, "All these dirty insides are usable. Some might be slightly green but don't worry, it's all usable . . ." He even scraped the meat from inside the two halves of upper protective head shell – but left the little sack found right at the top of the head. This is the creature's stomach. The grey fingery bits – the lungs – stuck to the sides of the leg section were also abandoned.

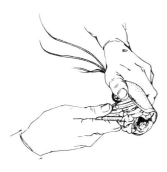

Pulling away legs and abdomen from carapace of lobster

"There will be hardly any meat in the legs themselves," he concluded, "so I won't bother to

pick them. Again, they will all be used later in the stock."

But not yet. For now the stock mix had been cooking for about twenty minutes and he pulled the pan off the gas and left it to cool.

The lobster bones he broke with a heavy knife, placed them in a shallow tin and set this in a medium oven just by themselves for twenty minutes or so. But don't worry. Baked lobster bones as such were not a part of the dish. It was all part of the plan to suck every ounce of taste from the ingredients – as we shall see later.

"I am now going to make the terrine proper," John announced.

His first move was to cut one whole, small onion into terribly fine pieces – "I need all this small because I want the final terrine to have a very fine texture. It's very important. A food processor isn't up to fine, fibrous material . . ."

The same rationale made him *crush* half a garlic clove with the flat of a knife, and then pare and crush six very thin slices of fresh ginger – throwing the outer skin to the side with the unused pile of brown onion skins.

Now John sniffed. He shouted, "Oh Christ, the oven hasn't lit . . ." And we took a break to enjoy the diverting drama of clearing the kitchen of gas. Personally, I remain grateful that the sensitive chef's nose picked up the taint in the air before we all went up with the lobster bones.

"The oven," John said finally, "is now alight."

Back to the terrine.

A heavy frying pan was reached for – heavy, John explained, because that allowed for proper heat distribution, avoiding the creation of "hot spots" to which the cooking food might stick. The squashed and chopped onion, garlic and ginger went into this pan together with a knob of butter, and fried hard.

As this cooked for a minute or so, John took half an orange and squeezed it into a dish: "For flavour and acid," he said. "Very important thing, acid. It brings out the flavour from the food . . . oh

my goodness . . ." He dashed back to rescue the frying pan from an impromptu hot spot. It was a day of dramas.

Now a little of the orange juice was thrown into the pan to "de-glaze", or remove the browned bits from the bottom, while he scraped with a spoon. Breaking briefly, John chopped the leaves and minor stalks from three good-sized twigs of parsley, reducing to a mash rather than fragments – and always keeping an eye and occasional spoon on the cooking onion and ginger.

Keeping back just a little of the lobster meat to use as chunks near the end, John then threw all the remaining meat into the frying pan – producing within a minute that definitively wonderful smell which proclaims real progress. After a further five minutes of cooking – perhaps ten minutes in total from the time the onion first went into the pan – John poured in half the remaining orange juice and a little pepper.

This thick stew he agitated and reduced. Why? "To concentrate the flavours and de-glaze," he explained.

Soon, it looked just like a handful of sludge.

Unperturbed by the sewage-like nature of the dish forming under his spoon, John explained, "I'm going for a stripy terrine. I had a vague idea at the beginning that I would do that, but I'm not sure exactly how the colours will look . . ."

The sludge came off the gas and was placed in a shallow water-bath to cool as John turned to the waiting skinned plaice fillets and cut them into small strips about a quarter of an inch wide and two inches long. "Watch for bones – you wouldn't want to choke the managing director . . ." Or yourself, for that matter.

Two-thirds of that chopped plaice was now placed into a large glass bowl, together with half a squashed garlic clove and five twists of black pepper.

With a comforting lack of elegance, John then – eventually – separated the yolks and whites of two eggs, adding the whites to the plaice mix and retaining the yolks. Most of the rest of the orange

juice followed – a dribble only, actually, though as John said, "Orange goes particularly well with lobster."

And finally, in went the most essential ingredient of all – the chopped parsley. Essential for colour, that is. For the whole whitish mix turned prettily green at this stage, and John explained, "What this is going to be is the outer layer, with the pink lobster layer inside."

This, you will understand, is why at this stage John had two very distinct parts to the meal: the green plaice mix (some of the fillets, remember, were still kept by) and the pink lobster sludge still cooling in the pan – cooling, it should be added, so that there would be no instant cooking effect later when the egg yolks were mixed in.

Now the green plaice underwent about thirty seconds in the food processor until it had the consistency of thick cream. A liquidiser will do the same job, apparently, but it takes a lot longer.

Leaving the mix in the processor for the moment, John next scooped about 4 fl oz of very thick double cream into a separate bowl and whipped it until his arm became tired and floppy. Then he folded in the plaice mix, tasted it, and declared, "It's a little bland. You should never be afraid to taste things raw, by the way, it's an essential part of cooking . . . This needs lemon." He squeezed in a little fresh juice, then declared, "Yes, that's bringing it up. Of course, the danger is that it will curdle – I just hope it won't . . ."

And it didn't. And that was the green part of the terrine completed. What remained was the all important pink stripe of lobster.

The thick, juicy lobster mix, mottled pink with coral or roe, was now converted into a kind of Heart Attack Special, with the addition in a bowl of two fluid ounces of single cream and the two left-over egg yolks, plus a final sprinkle of orange juice.

There is a wonderful story, recounted in Brewer's *Dictionary of Phrase and Fable* of the French chef Vatel who, preparing a feast at the

time of Louis XIV, was told that the lobsters for
his planned sauce had failed to arrive – upon which
this genius of the kitchen retired to his room and
ran a sword through his body. ("Died for want of
lobster sauce" is the phrase deriving from this
unfortunate incident.)

Watching John Kenward mix the riches of
cream and egg yolk with our humble beast I was
left wondering whether Vatel had not in fact
chosen merely the swifter of two options.

However, this vital-looking mix, now
combined with the remaining third of chopped
plaice fillets, went into the same unwashed food
processor bowl for a similar whisk round until
thoroughly creamed. "If the mix turns out too
runny it won't layer as I plan to do it," John
warned. "And if that does happen you just have to
cook the mixes separately. Putting them together
in a runny state will just make them merge."

But this was not a trap John fell into. His two
mixes were beautifully balanced – moist and yet
clinging to the touch.

Almost ready to bring the two halves
together, John first whipped another 4 fl oz of
thick cream and folded in the lobster mix, together
with the unused, cubed pieces of lobster flesh "for
bite". Again, he tasted the mix and this time added
a pinch of salt, pointing out that as the dish was to
be served cold it was better slightly to overdo salt
because the flavour yield dropped with the
temperature.

At last, the final act of this little cookery drama
was at hand.

John, of course, had a proper terrine in which
to do the baking – but you may not. In which case
use any oval or oblong dish you can safely heat up.

The terrine John used was about twelve
inches long, three inches wide and three deep. It
had a lid and was made of enamelled cast iron.
This he placed in a water-bath (a shallow, wide
tray containing an inch of water to prevent rapid
cooking). But first he carefully layered and
smoothed the two colourful mixes of fish. A
bottom layer of half the green, levelled with a

spoon, then all the pink mix – again, smoothed down. Finally, the other half of the green mix.

The cover went on, dish and water tray were then carried to a pre-heated oven (low to medium, about Gas Mark 3, 325°F, 170°C) and laid to rest.

It was almost finished.

The bones? Baked bones?

I forgot to mention these. In fact, after cooking for twenty minutes until rattly and crisp, they were crushed with a knife. A pot was set to heat, containing butter, chopped onion, the remaining onion skins, half a clove of crushed garlic, two shakes of turmeric, 12 crushed allspice berries, a little fresh marjoram, half a chopped carrot, a twig of chopped celery and about three slivers of fresh ginger. This selection of ingredients is governed partly by personal choice and partly by availability: but take care, says John, that nothing added to this sauce does more than contribute to an overall warmth and complexity of taste. No single ingredient should dominate or crowd out the lobster flavour.

Into this spluttering pan went the lobster bones, followed by plaice bones dredged from the separate stock, and about a dozen twists of black pepper.

After five minutes of further frying the whole collection was deluged with about a pint and a half of stock liquid (freeze the rest for use with another meal) and simmered for fifteen minutes. Then the liquid was strained and put by for reducing and mixing with a little cream and fresh parsley when needed – hot – for the cold terrine.

That terrine took an hour and twenty minutes to cook – but it was tested regularly, sometimes by plunging a small knife into the centre and feeling the blade to see if the heart was yet warm or cold.

Whatever you do, don't let the terrine dry out. As John said, it must be firm, puffy and moist – there can even be clear liquid on the surface as that dries with chilling. If anything, undercook.

And when, finally, you turn this out, easing it

with a spatula to a plate for cutting into thin slices and serving, pouring on the warm sauce, picking mouthfuls with a delicate fork . . . you will become almost alarmed at how marvellously you have done to produce such a thing.

John left his terrine to chill for several hours, so that when my fork at last plunged into this complex mix of taste and texture it was late at night, the restaurant outside was in full swing, the atmosphere was of bustle and movement and clattered plates. It didn't matter.

The terrine was light on the tongue like shredded ice-cream, mottled, as John had planned, with the surprise of sudden lobster flecks. The sauce was strong, spicy and hot with the tang of salty lobster, and for the first time in years I wanted to pick up the plate at the end, and lick it.

No time.

John and I were discussing variations.

VARIATIONS

OTHER TERRINES: It seems that the first thing to remember about a terrine is that, at heart, it is an ironical contradiction. It is both a very special dish, and at the same time it can be a money-saver for anyone who buys a little too much of something and stashes that something away in the freezer for some future occasion that so rarely arrives.

As John explained, "I often make terrine to use up left-overs and frozen fish – the only circumstance under which I would use any frozen fish. Because what is spoilt most by freezing is the texture, and the texture in a terrine is not important because it is bashed into small pieces.

"For instance, today there was frozen mussel meat on sale at the fish shop and I could easily have used that instead of the lobster to save money."

How?

He explained at once, "Fried the meat with some onion but cut the mussels a little to get rid of as much moisture as possible. I'd have ignored the

stripy bit and just whizzed it all together –
possibly using lemon sole instead of plaice, but it
wouldn't have mattered. And I'd have used whole
egg instead of separating because there would
have been no colour difference."

Was that all?

John shrugged. "I'd have used more parsley
because mussels would have produced a khaki
effect which isn't very appealing."

Was there anything else he could have done to
overcome the dullness of brown mussels?

"I could have lightly poached one plaice fillet,
removed the liquid and put that in the middle of the
terrine."

In those circumstances, of course, you would
make sure that for cutting the terrine you used a
very sharp knife – or squashing might result.

Smoked salmon, John went on, would make a
"brilliant" addition to a terrine. He proposed using
slices cut from the tail end of a salmon side, or
even taken from a packet. The terrine dish would
then be lightly buttered and the slices pasted
round the inside as a total cover. Other pieces of
smoked salmon could then go in with the plaice or
lemon sole and food-processed as before.

The ideas are instant and endless. But it is
perhaps in this area above all that the most
interesting advances and discoveries can be made,
not in a chef's kitchen, but at home.

Here, meanwhile, are condensed details of the
terrine and sauce John made on this day:

LOBSTER TERRINE
As a starter for 8-10

¾ lb (350 g) lobster

2 lb (900 g) whole plaice

butter

garlic

fresh ginger

2 small onions

½ orange

pepper

2 eggs

½ lemon

3 parsley sprigs

7 fl oz (200 ml) double cream

2 fl oz (55 ml) single cream
(you could use all double cream for convenience)

Salt

1   Pick the lobster meat. Fillet and skin the plaice.

2   Heat in a pan one knob of butter, plus crushed half garlic clove and crushed slices of ginger, and a small chopped onion.

3   Add a squeeze of orange juice plus all the lobster (chopped) except a few chunks kept for later.

4   Cook and mix for ten minutes, adding half the remaining orange juice and twists of pepper. Reduce.

5   Cool the pan, meanwhile cut small strips from plaice, putting two-thirds into bowl with half a squashed garlic clove and five twists of black pepper.

6   Separate the eggs. Add the whites to the plaice with a little more orange juice and some chopped parsley.

7   Food process for about 30 seconds. Whip 4 fl oz thick cream and gently fold in the plaice mix. Taste and add lemon juice.

8   Add egg yolks to the cooled lobster mix plus two fluid ounces of single cream and a final sprinkle of orange juice, also the remaining third of plaice fillets.

9   Food process for about thirty seconds. Whip 4 fl oz of thick cream and fold into lobster mix.

10   Add chopped lobster bits "for bite".

11   Layer and bake in oven (Gas Mark 3, 325°F, 170°C) for up to an hour and twenty minutes, but test regularly. Use a water-bath to prevent rapid cooking.

LOBSTER SAUCE

For the stock
plaice bones and skin
onion, finely chopped
parsley stalks
celery or fennel
½ clove garlic
water

lobster bones
butter
chopped onion
onion skins
½ clove garlic
2 shakes turmeric
12 crushed allspice berries
little fresh marjoram
½ chopped carrot
twig of chopped celery
approx 3 slivers fresh ginger
cream and parsley
black pepper

1   Make a stock from the listed ingredients and set to simmer.

2   Break lobster bones and put in a medium oven for twenty minutes.

3   Mix rest of ingredients with lobster bones.

4   Heat, and add plaice bones from stock mix plus twelve twists of black pepper. After five minutes add pint and a half of stock.

5   Simmer for fifteen minutes.

6   Strain, reduce and finally add a little cream and parsley.

MACKEREL WITH GOOSEBERRY SAUCE

SMOKED MACKEREL SALAD

A broken tooth was the inspiration for this dish: a single molar which snapped in our chef's mouth while he was eating something which, presumably, he did not cook himself. This left us with only a very short time in which John could create a dish before dashing in pain to the dentist.

We could have cancelled the meal, of course, but even as we considered this we stumbled upon the obvious truth that small emergencies arise in every household almost every week. Therefore it would be silly of us to try and duck our own. So this dish is dedicated to those times when minutes are almost as important as the food itself. And the strange fact is that although the whole meal took well under twenty minutes to prepare it was an outstanding success.

The brief, then, through force of circumstances alone, was to produce a lightning meal for two or more.

Partly for speed, but also for the sake of trying something different, John decided as we walked down the hill to the fish shop that he would try and cook whole fish this time rather than involve himself in too much fancy preparation. (Actually, on reflection, we weren't "walking" down the hill at all. John, propelled by the urgency of his broken tooth, was gambolling out in front like a dog on a lead.)

We arrived and found – almost luckily – that there were few whole fish in the window that day, so the time devoted to choosing was cut very short. John glanced, said, "Mackerel – I think with gooseberries," and we went inside.

Once there, of course, whim took a small hand and he added a further fillet of smoked mackerel to the two selected fresh fish – but by the time we were back on the street again he had put this additional purchase into a menu slot: the ingredient for a salad to go with the main dish.

It ought to be said here that John's decision to cook mackerel with gooseberries (a fairly classic coupling) was prompted by the fact that he always tries to use food in season. Food changes with the year and it makes sense not to fight it, he believes: "It's nice to embrace the seasons. Gooseberries which are good for sauces are available between mid-June and July. The dessert gooseberries which come later are richer and lack the astringency, which is what you are looking for."

Not to say that you cannot attempt this style of dish at other times of the year – a point we shall come to later – but that the purest taste is available in June and July. A key point to bear in mind is that you are looking for a sharp contrast, the astringency of the fruit against the oily flavour of the mackerel.

And mackerel *is* a powerful tasting fish. Not as rich as herring, but almost as distinctive, almost as overwhelming. Personally I find it very enjoyable, and it has the built-in advantage that you can always tell if a mackerel is old: not only does its belly sag and the flesh hang loose, but that

Mackerel

wonderful blue-green zig-zag pattern which marks out its back and sides dulls quickly with age to a matt blur.

On the other hand, when mackerel are fresh – as ours were – the pattern shines, and the creature feels as hard as a bullet.

Of course, the sad thing about the beast is that although it is very easy for our fishermen to catch it (it is nicknamed "the suicide fish" because of the way it tends to throw itself into nets) the British themselves are suspicious of the mackerel. They won't buy nearly enough of this massive resource, and so Britain sells them cheaply to the East Europeans while we busy ourselves importing the more attractive, yet more expensive, cod. So next time you are staring in at a fishmonger's window, remember our balance of payments.

Back to the day.

In we went to the greengrocer's a few doors along the road and there we met Billy, the young owner, who asked politely about our book and sold us cut-rate gooseberries from a box of wonderful fruit concealed in a storeroom at the back. Mozart, receiving gold from a patron, felt no more emotional than we did at this gesture of support. Certainly we cashed in on the price cut by adding a fine bunch of watercress to the bill.

"For the salad," John decided. "It will mix with the smoked mackerel."

At last, breathless in the restaurant kitchen, we began rummaging through cupboards to find the very few other staple ingredients which would complete the basis of the meal. A lemon, one onion, butter, some salt, black pepper and sugar.

"We could have this cold," said John, turning for knife and chopping-board. "It will probably take fifteen minutes or so to cook and then it can be eaten at any time – hot or cold."

What happened next was a tooth-propelled blur which almost defeated my ability to make notes, but it is best here to consider what happened in a slower style, because there *are* mistakes to be made if you are not careful.

BASIC PREPARATION

John's first move was to peel and finely chop a small onion – discarding the rough cuts because this time there was to be no stock. Mackerel itself makes poor stock, which, as John pointed out, is another good reason for using the creature whole: the bones would only go to waste otherwise. You may also like to note that *cooked* fish bones turn smelly less quickly than raw ones: a bonus for your rubbish bin.

The chopped onion, John put into a small saucepan with a generous knob of butter, which was then set on a high gas.

The half-pound of gooseberries went on top, just as they were: "I won't do anything to them because I know I will be sieving them later," John explained.

While this heated up he turned on the oven to medium hot (Gas Mark 5, 375°F, 190°C) and began to process the two waiting mackerel.

This was a straightforward procedure because all that was required was the gutting or "cleaning" of the fish, and then the removal of their heads. If, however, it is the first time you have attempted such an operation you may react a little squeamishly to the first slice of the knife. Bear up, and do it this way, for all "round" fish like mackerel, herring, trout and so on: push a sharp-pointed knife into the tiny cavity towards the tail end of the fish on its underbelly; thrust upwards until your knife touches the backbone, and then draw the blade firmly along towards the head.

When you reach where the chin would be if fish had these things, stop and scrape out everything inside. You may find it easier to trap the intestines against the chopping-board with the flat of the knife, then pull the fish to one side. The only danger, as John pointed out, is that simply cleaning a fish often leaves the backbone blood in place – and it is essential to remove that: "It tastes terribly bitter and can ruin the meal," said John.

He pushed out this thick, black blood with one finger, then ran the fish under the tap for a final clean. Finally, the head came off with one Mikado-

like sweep of the knife just below the gill slits.

For a few moments now, John considered "slashing" the sides of the mackerel in order to make them cook quicker – a useful technique, he explained, particularly when you want to mix the accompanying flavour into the flesh of the fish.

Yet because these particular creatures were not thick enough to require too much cooking John decided against cutting them. He simply placed them in a baking dish, added knobs of butter along the sides of the fish, plus a twist or two of black pepper, and placed them in the pre-heated oven.

During this time, of course, he had been returning to the gas stove to give the occasional prod and stir to the gooseberry mix, to which he now added about half a cup of cold water. When the pan boiled he turned down the gas and set it to simmer.

After a minute or two more, John began tentatively squashing the gooseberries to see if they were cooked, and when they were soft he became more robust with the spoon, churning the mix around and adding a pinch of salt.

"Mackerel," he said as he worked, "is the sort of fish I would like to cook at home, but I don't cook it in the restaurant because it needs to be very fresh and you have to sell it on the night you buy it. It won't hold over."

Smoked mackerel, on the other hand, will keep for several days, and if you are lucky you will be able to buy some that has not been dyed. Not that dye affects the keeping power of the fish: it's just unnecessary.

Like much of the smoked fish eaten by the British, vast quantities of these fillets are coloured to make them look more attractive in the shop – regardless of the fact that the resultant effect is more suggestive of Windscale glow than a jolly good tuck in.

The trouble is that too many people have fallen for this simple marketing trick and have built the idea of beacon-bright smoked fish into their concept of the product as it should be. Selling smoked fish I would offer both dyed and undyed to

customers and would explain to anyone who seemed uncertain that the yellow fish contained a colouring and the slightly paler fillets did not. Many would still choose the yellow. Once when this happened I quietly excused myself, walked out to my office at the back of the shop, and punched a hole in the wall. Patience is a virtue which demands sacrifices.

John, meanwhile, was skinning his smoked mackerel.

It was a quick job. He gently cut right down the middle of the fillet but did not slice through the skin itself. Then he gently folded the meat back and pulled it away from the skin. Finally, he broke the meat into bite-sized pieces, making a small though not exhaustive attempt to ferret out the left-over bones: "I won't be too careful about it because it's a bony meal anyway." The pile of meat he set by for a minute or two; the skin and bones, he threw away.

Less than ten minutes had passed since the gooseberry sauce had been set to cook and by now it was done. John poured the mix into a sieve over a small bowl and pushed and prodded until all the liquid was through and dull green sludge was left in the sieve, the bottom of which he scraped to recapture the thickness for the sauce.

In went a finger. A lick. "Bitter, isn't it? I'm wondering whether it needs a little bit of sugar . . ."

Reaching for the Tate and Lyle, John went on, "It's very important to cook and taste like this, you can't tell otherwise how sweet it will be. You have to wait until it is cooked and then see what comes out. You are not after a sweet sauce as such, of course, but something which will cut through into the fish. That's where the combination is good – mackerel and gooseberry, like cod and vinegar. You want something not quite as bitter as lemon, but not far off . . ."

As an aside, if you need any confirmation that mackerel and gooseberry were created specifically to complement one another on a plate you need look no further than the French

language. The French for gooseberry is *groseille à maquereau* where *groseille* is a currant, and *maquereau* is . . . well, I'm sure you know. The point is that the culinary link is ingrained in the language itself.

Seeking exactly the right zest for his sauce, John added two teaspoons of white sugar, stirred it then tasted again and added one more teaspoon, after which he said he was satisfied. I tried it myself then, and while the taste is always difficult to describe this could safely be called fruity and sharp, but just off being tart. It had a freshness. It was not stewed.

Pouring this thick custard-like mix into a ramekin for serving, John took a few seconds to toss the smoked mackerel into the fridge, followed by the watercress, which he had placed in water first.

It was a small but significant piece of thoughtfulness. As John explained, "I shall be mixing the smoked fish and watercress together but I won't do that until we're going to eat because that would make the leaves go soggy. I'll keep them both cold meanwhile."

Just over fifteen minutes had passed since the fresh fish had gone into the oven, and by now a prod with the finger showed the flesh to be firm but flakey. Effectively, the meal was ready, but John pointed to one danger which even earlier caution had missed: round the neck of one fish a little blood still clung to the backbone. "Taste it," he ordered. I did so, and, reproaching the cook with a glance, retreated to the sink in order to wash out my mouth. It was dreadful. Do remove this backbone blood when you are cooking fish.

When everything had finally cooled, and John had returned cheerfully from the dentist, we sat down and prepared to eat. John mixed the watercress and smoked mackerel, adding fresh lemon juice and a little black pepper, but no oil. "There's oil in the smoked mackerel," he said. The gooseberry sauce we spooned in green pools onto the white of our plates; the fresh mackerel we eased from the bones with the flat of a knife,

and prepared to share our food with the snatching hands of visiting kitchen helpers.

The day was sunny and warm. We set tables in the beautifully cultivated garden courtyard at the back of the restaurant, where honeysuckle clambered over old red brickwork and goldfish moved through the waters of an ornamental pond, unaware of the carnage offered to their sea-born, plate-landed cousins nearby.

Above all, the meal was impressive for the levels of change and interest it contained: the gooseberry sauce added a lovely summery fruitiness to the heaviness of the mackerel, the smoked fish and watercress provided an underlay of comfortable warmth. Very seasonal. And, of course, very quick. For the whole dish had involved little more time than it takes harassed parents to heat up some beans on toast. It was the closest John would ever get to the convenience of a hamburger – and for speed, it wasn't far off. For taste, it made me wonder, sitting in the sunshine, sipping iced lemon water, why anybody ever bothered with so-called fast food.

We cleared everything. And then we discussed what else might have been attempted.

VARIATIONS

The most important point to deal with, of course, is the fact that John would not make a savoury gooseberry sauce outside the months of June or July. As he pointed out while shopping, the fruit becomes too sweet later in the year and is more suitable for desserts. So an alternative base for the sauce is essential if you are to try this meal outside those two key months.

John proposed using slightly under-ripe, or certainly quite young, tomatoes – going through the method exactly as with gooseberries, but possibly cutting down on sugar at the end. Good months for this version, he said, would be August and September.

But redcurrants would also work well. "They don't have a very pronounced flavour but they are quite astringent and would be a good alternative," said John. "Or, of course, you could do away with

a sauce and simply use sour cream or yoghurt instead – just by itself. But you would need a good, sharp yoghurt, preferably made with goat's milk. A standard supermarket yoghurt isn't really what I would look for."

But keeping with the gooseberry sauce, wasn't it possible to uprate the whole meal a little further? To make it a really special dish?

"Yes – make it with salmon instead of mackerel and serve it hot," John said. "You could also cook the gooseberries in a fish stock if you had any, then sieve them out and add cream towards the end. It would make a beautiful sauce – just pour it round the baked fillets or steaks baked in butter."

What about using the sauce to cook with?

"You could do that," John agreed. "I've done it with bass and gooseberries in the past – cutting terribly thin slices of fish at an oblique angle to the skin, then poach these in a stock with gooseberries in and some butter; cook it gently on the top until the fish is done, which will only take a few moments, then take out the bass and go on cooking the sauce until the gooseberries are cooked right through. Then sieve them or not, depending on how refined you want it to be, and add a little more butter. You could do that with salmon very well, too."

But when pressed for further, perhaps more exciting ways of using mackerel itself, John shook his head.

"The simpler you cook something like that the better it is," he insisted. "Mackerel is a very cheap fish and rightly so – it's not grand. It is very nice but it isn't something that merits great attention lavished on it beyond doing something simple, such as baking it with strips of bacon."

A reminder now of the way to cook the meal we tried that day.

MACKEREL WITH GOOSEBERRY SAUCE
Ingredients for 2

2 × 12 oz (700 g) medium-sized fresh mackerel
1 small onion
knob of butter
½ lb (225 g) gooseberries
sugar
salt, black pepper

1   Clean the mackerel, being sure to wash out the spinal blood. Chop off the heads. Pre-heat the oven, medium to high.

2   Chop the onion, add a knob of butter, place in a pan and heat, pouring untrimmed gooseberries on top, later adding half a cup of water.

3   Put knobs of butter on the fish, place them in a baking dish and twist on some pepper. Put in the warmed oven.

4   Stir the gooseberry mix occasionally, testing to see if the fruit has gone squashy. Add a pinch of salt.

5   When gooseberries are cooked, stir the mix thoroughly, and sieve into a bowl. Add sugar to taste but do not make it sweet.

6   Test mackerel after fifteen minutes. When cooked but firm, serve hot or cold, using the sauce as a side dip.

SMOKED MACKEREL SALAD
Ingredients for 2

10 -12 oz (275 -350 g) smoked mackerel
small bunch of watercress
½ lemon
black pepper

1   Pull the skin from the smoked mackerel, sift for bones then break into bite-sized pieces.

2   Mix in the watercress, add the lemon juice and pepper. Serve. But do not mix the watercress and fish until just before you plan to eat.

6

SKATE FILLETS IN VINE LEAVES

We prayed for squid this time.

Odd, isn't it, how even the sternest of rules can eventually be broken by the very people who make them up in the first place? This whole book is dedicated to the idea of deciding what fish to cook *after* you have seen what is on display. And yet today we went shopping for squid.

The full truth is that John was aware that a local fishing boat had landed some of these creatures the day before, and he was dying to try some. His opportunity seemed assured when I suggested that this time he might cook something different, something slightly unusual. "Squid," he retorted. And we set off.

We should have known better – for by the time we got to the fish shop all the squid had been sold, and John was left dry-eyed but emotional, facing disappointment and a sudden need to rely solely on his wits. Serves you right, you might snap. And I do not suppose that either of us would argue.

What happened, however, was not only a vindication of the whole "don't buy till you see" theme, but a voyage into experimentation which worked on a number of levels: we had an excellent meal, John was encouraged to use home-grown ingredients (which raised an interesting point of

freshness), and he made discoveries arising from criticisms which were made at the end of it all.

But more about all that later. In the fish shop, John picked on skate, that gorgeous, reddish brown fish which looks something like a bloodied fan and very little like any kind of fish. It is, in fact, the edible side parts of the ray, and John picked it this time mainly because the specimens on show looked good and thick and in excellent condition; but also because he suddenly thought it would be good to try a firm fish like this in combination with some vine leaves which he remembered were currently sprouting in his garden at home.

As with the chapter on mackerel and gooseberries, the theme of seasonality arose with his decision to use vine leaves. The vine season for cooking is short – July to September – because beyond these times the leaves become too thick to wrap anything in except your tool kit. John's view, put simply, is that you should grab these things while you can.

More clearly, his attitude to the whole subject of seasons is summed up in his flat refusal to use dried herbs of any kind – something which most ordinary kitchens possess in large quantities.

John says, "I never use dried herbs – full stop. Why? Because they taste like straw."

A daunting view. Could it not be limiting, especially for a professional cook?

"No it isn't you silly person," (a cascade of good-natured laughter) "it extends the range of other possibilities. It makes you consider other things . . .

"So in the winter you don't use fresh herbs because they are not around, you use vegetables, citrus fruits, mixtures of fish as ways of getting the variety of taste. Then there's spice – ginger, pepper, even dried fruit – they make wonderful sauces . . ."

Cooks, he urged, should "embrace the seasons", relying as far as possible on the good things which the calendar has to offer rather than making sacrifices of taste in order to take things out of time.

Perhaps this is a view which cannot be wholly adopted by the home cook, but the least that could be done, John felt, was the establishment of a small herb garden in each back yard. That way, the seasons would stare cooks in the face every day.

But, of course, you have to be practical. So back up the hill John gathered a handful of young vine leaves from home – a couple of hundred yards from the restaurant – but though he was also thinking of using parsley he left his own where it lay in the ground: "It's gone to seed," he admitted. He went and bought some in a shop.

The idea for the meal, John explained as he finally surveyed all the produce back in the restaurant kitchen, was to wrap the skate in vine leaves and make a parsley stuffing. But the precise way in which this would happen came to him only gradually, as the meal went ahead.

Why use leaves, I asked?

"There are two reasons: the first is that it does add a very good flavour, and the second is that you are cooking the fish in a way which allows nothing to escape – no juices or aroma."

It is interesting to hear John use highly descriptive words like "aroma" when discussing his own food. Very often they come out with a laughing emphasis, as if he is embarrassed by their strength. In fact, he admits to finding the English language unwieldy for food use and I imagine he has a point: why else would foreign terms like *al dente* be dragged in to help?

Certainly I used to struggle in the shop when asked (as happened a dozen times a day) to describe the taste of a certain kind of fish. Take skate: it is a stronger taste than, say, cod, but weaker than mackerel. Beyond that it's . . . well; you are left comparing it with something else, like huss only not as strong. I know a fishmonger who would fall back on "tasty" all the time – anything from bass to sea urchins. Jolly tasty.

Back in the kitchen, I asked John what people should do if they did not have access to a handy vine.

"You could use spinach," he said.

"Or lettuce," chipped in Christine, one of John's helpers who was drifting through the kitchen humming snatches from a Verdi opera (all his helpers are like that).

"Or lettuce," John repeated.

Cabbage he had also tried, but found it too brittle – "A bloody pain" in fact.

And now what?

"I'll fillet the skate," said John.

The idea of filleting skate may surprise many cooks. To put it into context, skate is a cartilaginous creature, which means it has a softish, rubbery frame rather than a hard bony one, and it is traditional therefore to cook and eat the flesh still on the skeleton: a classic recipe is to fry skate in brown butter with a thread of vinegar, after which it can be eaten with just a fork as the flesh slides easily off the cartilage. John's decision to fillet before cooking, therefore, was an unusual move.

But a word of warning here: whatever you do with your skate, never let your fishmonger sell it to you with the skin on. The biggest and most troublesome of these delicious creatures are protected by huge hooks in a rough skin and this combination is capable of ripping nasty holes in an unwary hand.

In the shop I would try and buy in only skate which had already been skinned, giving some other poor dolt the taste of his own blood. But I was not always successful and the groans from staff confronted with two stone of these brutes to deal with at seven thirty in the morning were audible all down the high street.

So beware. A soft white skin on the "bottom" of the wing is acceptable, but never the top – unless you are terribly good with a knife.

On this day, our two wings had already been skinned, making the task all the easier.

BASIC
PREPARATION

First John placed a knife against the "top" or thick end of the fish at the point where the flesh gives way to a final, thin ridge of bone or cartilage. Then

Cutting away flesh of
skate wing

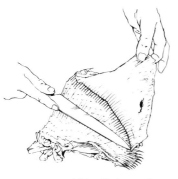

Lifting flesh away from
bones and trimming edge
from skate fillet

he sliced down the fan shape, pulling back the flesh and disclosing the semi-transparent frame beneath. Peeling and pulling he removed one complete side of flesh, turned the wing over and did the same to the other, slightly thinner side.

Because the resulting fillets were so large, John cut each one in half, producing slices two to two-and-a-half inches wide – but you may or may not want to do this, depending on the size of the fish you are able to buy.

"It's so easy to fillet skate I don't know why it isn't done more often," said John. "I have sometimes cut half-way down the top fillet and tucked in parsley or lemon or whatever with some butter and baked it; that works wonderfully."

Baked it covered or uncovered – for wasn't skate a notoriously "dry" fish?

John nodded. "Rub butter on the top," he said, "and then try baking it uncovered, but keep an eye on it and watch for drying. I will sometimes do either but it depends partly on how thin the meat is as to whether it will dry out, and partly on how hot the oven is – even where in the oven you put the fish. The main point is you keep an eye on these things."

What now?

"Well, I could make a sandwich of these fillets, with a stuffing in the middle . . . but they look as if they will roll quite well, so I'll try that . . ."

And the fish went into the fridge while John got on with the rest of the preparation. Keeping fish cool at such moments, he said, was a good habit to get into, as it maintained the quality of the flesh.

The bones from the skate went into a stock pot with one sliced and crushed garlic clove, a pint of water, and the inside rough leaves from a small onion (the outside brown skin was thrown away).

The onion itself was finely sliced ("Cut pole to pole," John warned, "cross-cut onion rings don't break up so well and can be chewy") and these pieces were put with a knob of butter into another

pan. Now both saucepans were set to heat, the stock on high, the onion rather lower.

Next, John took the stalks off the fresh parsley, leaving about one ounce of florets. The stalks were chopped and added to the stock, while the florets were very finely minced with a sharp knife – chopped again and again – and put to one side.

After that, he turned to the vine leaves.

"These are actually nice fine young leaves," said John, "so I will only take off the stalks. If they were any bigger I would slice out that central vein. But not this time. Now I have to blanch them."

Yet another pan – this containing about half an inch of water – was set to boil, and as soon as this was achieved the leaves were thrown in and turned once, cooking for a total of about thirty seconds in all.

"This softens them so that I can do the wrapping," John explained, spooning the leaves from the pan, spreading them carefully onto a chopping-board, dabbing them dry with a cloth.

To the gently simmering onion and butter he now added two crushed garlic cloves, and after a further three minutes or so – about ten minutes cooking time in all – he took the onion off the gas. Now he turned the oven on to a medium heat (Gas Mark 5, 375°F, 190°C) for using later, and onto each cooked vine leaf placed a small nut of butter which he rubbed over the surface with a finger, and a twist of black pepper.

Two things to bear in mind here. The first is that John always uses unsalted butter so that he has some control over how much salt goes into a dish. The second is that if you have a very sensitive palate you might ease up a little on the amount of pepper you use. John put a lot into this meal, and the result was delightfully powerful. You will possibly want to experiment and make your own judgment.

Meanwhile, a lot more black pepper was being added to the onion, together with the minced parsley, and the whole lot stirred into a fine mulch faintly resembling something you spread on the

garden. This mix was not reheated.

John now tinkered briefly with the fridge-rescued skate fillets, reminding himself by rolling, patting and turning the things over exactly what he might do with them.

At last he disclosed that it would be best to put the parsley and onion filling next to what had been the inside of each fillet – a side more likely to absorb the flavour as it had only just been cut.

So a fat dab of parsley filling was added to each fillet in this way, and the flesh rolled up from the thin end leaving a chunky lip along the side of every piece.

Finally, John carefully placed each rolled fillet into the centre of a vine leaf, bringing up the back leaf-flaps, tucking in the sides, and making a perfect little swiss roll of each one. They were placed, leaf-joint downwards, into an open, buttered tray, and more butter was gently smeared on the top of each roll, together with a little more pepper (see what I mean about the pepper? It was all over the place). The dish was put uncovered into the pre-heated oven.

Sauce and vegetables were all that remained to be done before we ate.

The bubbling stock was strained into another pan and set on a high gas to reduce. I asked John if he ever used flour to thicken sauces and he said that it might sometimes happen at home, but never in the restaurant: "It can blanket the flavour," he said. "People are paying for what they get here, but at home you might not have such a good stock or you might not have the time to reduce it properly, so I have used it there. Sometimes I'll use cream to thicken."

Pondering the vegetable rack we found little to get excited about beyond a few carrots and some odds and ends.

"Courgettes would be nice," I suggested.

"Yes," said John and helpers Christine and Jenny with one voice. So I had to go and buy some.

Five minutes later John was slicing four

Parsley filling on skate fillet – starting to roll from narrow end

Rolling skate fillet round filling

Rolled skate fillet being wrapped in blanched vine leaf

Stuffed skate fillet wrapped in vine leaf

carrots and four large courgettes into matchstick thin pieces, meanwhile putting on to heat a pan containing a knob of butter, half a crushed garlic, ten twists of pepper and a generous splash of olive oil. The oil, by the way, raised the temperature of the cooking essence so that the vegetables could cook quicker and be correspondingly crisper; it also added flavour.

By now the fish had been cooking for twenty-five minutes, and a prod with a finger proved them firm and ready – so John put them above the stove to keep warm while he finished the vegetables and sauce.

To the reducing stock he added liquor from the cooked fish, plus juice from half a lemon.

The stick-like carrots were flung into the butter and oil mix and cooked and stirred for a minute or two before being joined by the courgettes together with a little chopped fresh marjoram and some chopped parsley. With much tossing and turning the whole lot was cooked for three to four minutes.

At the same time the sauce was tasted, another knob of butter was added, and boiling down continued. At the end of the three or four minutes vegetable-cooking time the whole meal was ready: the lovely red and green mix of carrots and courgettes at one end of each plate, the dull khaki of the rolled skate at the other, and the thickened sauce poured between (never over the food, which only confuses tastes).

It looked exciting and it tasted so. The slightly crisped outer vine leaves added a zest which provided a counterpoint to the slightly heavier, more subdued parsley and onion filling; and the pepper, of course, gave overall power. The vegetables were crisp and fresh. I am tempted to call the whole lot "tasty", but shan't.

There were four of us at the table – me, John, Christine and Jenny – and as we ate, a debate began over how firm or even chewy the vine leaves should be. John maintained that he wanted the leaves to be firm, but conceded that occasionally "they did go on a bit" in the mouth –

probably a reluctant concession, because the leaves really did have a fine, concentrated flavour.

Suggestions were made that he might have covered the rolled skate when baking – or perhaps steaming might have produced a more yielding texture. It was an interesting question which, in the end, we decided to put to the test.

So we finished the meal and agreed that whatever minor observations had been raised these were really only technical queries. Whatever happened now, the pioneering meal had been delightful and absorbing.

But the next morning we took the idea a little further. John cooked two different kinds of fish – salmon and turbot – using three kinds of leaves – vine, lettuce and spinach beet – and three kinds of cooking method: some he steamed, some he baked with a cover, and some he baked uncovered. Terribly complicated, of course, and no one would be helped by a detailed analysis of the results (anyway, it all got too much for my note-taking ability let alone my intellect). But some broad and interesting points arose from this trial.

The first was that a marvellous meal could be made simply by wrapping two-inch by one-inch strips of fish in leaves, together with a little pepper and butter and nothing else – as starters particularly, or for a picnic or even sliced as snacks.

Also, the steamed turbot in spinach proved a tremendous success – the fish so lightly cooked (suspended in a sieve over boiling water in a covered saucepan for just ten minutes) that it glistened with mother-of-pearl colours when sliced, the flavours of fish and spinach merging beautifully.

Beyond this, it was generally felt that steaming lettuce or vine leaves added very little to a dish. Lettuce turns flabby and papery, whereas vine leaves become tough.

Baking the leaves covered worked well with both lettuce and spinach, but seemed to make the vine leaves tough once more. But the original

version of baking uncovered had a pleasant effect on all leaves and all fish. Though a safe conclusion might be that cooking this way in a slow, middling heat is better than rushing things on a high gas.

It all sounds rather complicated if you have not lived through the cooking, and you may like to try some experiments of your own. If not, do have a go at steaming turbot fillets in spinach. Beyond that, bake your leaves slowly and, preferably, uncovered.

VARIATIONS

My first question was whether or not the strips of fish used in the second experiment could have been improved in any way. John thought that a little ginger might have been added to some of the fillets, and rather more butter. He was not in favour of making the portions any smaller, for that, he pointed out, would make the taste of the outer leaves rather more important, possibly overwhelming the fish.

Returning to the original meal, John felt that substituting cod fillets for skate would make a pleasant alternative, even though cod has slightly less flavour.

But more interesting than this, he thought, would be to take long strips of salmon fillet and paste them with puréed spinach, butter, salt and a point of garlic: "Spread that on and roll up the salmon and then roll the pieces in spinach leaf," he said. "Then bake them – I wouldn't cover them. I think it would make a very good first course."

But if a cook wanted to be more adventurous, using the contrasts of skate against flat fish would be an effective meal.

"Skate is good to mix with brill, lemon sole or even mussels," said John. "It's good because it has a pronounced character of its own which makes a nice contrast to the other fish. It seems somehow to have a flavour in between flat fish and round fish.

"If I had small skate wings, for instance, I would bake them whole with a fillet of lemon sole and perhaps one other fish, something cheap like

grey mullet – possibly a piece of salmon. You would make a sauce with the lemon sole bones, cook the mussels separately and throw them into the sauce at the end after you'd reduced the stock and added butter, lemon, parsley or tarragon. One small skate wing per person and a little of the other fish each. Marvellous."

But meanwhile here, for the confused at heart, is a final reminder of the dish which started all this.

SKATE FILLETS IN VINE LEAVES
Ingredients for 4

2 large, thick skate wings

1 pint (570 ml) water

1 small onion

3 garlic cloves

knob of butter

pepper

6 × 6-inch (15 cm) vine leaves

½ lemon

(1 lb (450 g) courgettes, few carrots, with a little
  marjoram and parsley – to accompany the meal)

1. Fillet the skate and add the bones to water (1 pint), together with onion leaves, crushed garlic clove and chopped parsley stalks in a stock pot. Keep fish cool. Boil the stock.

2. Chop an onion, add to butter in saucepan and heat.

3. Cut stalks from vine leaves, also the central vein if thick. Blanch for thirty seconds.

4. Add two crushed garlic cloves to the butter and onion. Cook for further two or three minutes, remove from heat. Total cooking time: about ten minutes.

5. Add butter and pepper to centre of each vine leaf – spreading with finger.

6   Add black pepper and finely chopped parsley to cooled onion mix. Stir well.

7   Add a little of this mix to each slice of skate fillet and roll up from the thin end. Place each rolled fillet on a vine leaf and roll again.

8   Place in a buttered dish, leaf-joint downwards. Bake in a pre-heated oven at about Gas Mark 5 (375°F, 190°C).

9   Strain the stock, reduce, add the juice of half a lemon plus a generous knob of butter.

10   Slice carrots and halved courgettes finely, fry carrots for two minutes in a mix of butter, olive oil, garlic, parsley and fresh marjoram, then add courgettes for two minutes more.

7

Dover Sole in Raspberry and Sage Sauce

On reflection, it was an odd day to choose for an outing to the coast.

The wind was only just easing after twenty-four hours of solid effort, so we knew even as we set off on the ten-mile drive to Newhaven that local fish was going to be scarce. I suppose we went for the change. Also because many people drive to the sea for a day out and come back with an unexpected fish dinner – so we thought we ought to try too.

The shop we chose in Newhaven was right on the harbour: not so much a shop, actually, more a single storey shed with big grey boxes of fish lined up on a wet concrete floor.

Marks and Spencer might have had little to learn about display from this set-up, but for sheer atmosphere it took some beating: a lot of ice, a little colour, a smell of seawater and fishing nets. And just outside, landing stages leading down to the boats themselves, shifting uneasily on a low tide.

If there was ever a time when a person felt they *must* buy fish it was now, against this sort of background.

But what fish?

We prowled the boxes like selective cats: a little skate here, some dabs, a cluster of grey-black flounders, Dover sole, a sudden blaze of lobster – cooked and red – and some rather old cod fillets. Not much else.

The wind had indeed taken its toll, but I was not about to raise an eyebrow of complaint. There were too many times in my own shop when customers were unable to see the link between poor weather and the lack of fish. Gales might scythe across Britain; storms might rage; yet in they would walk with their wellies and inside-out umbrellas, shaking water from their eyebrows and asking why the show was so poor today.

Because, because . . .

Well, not everybody was like that. But it *was* a problem.

In fact, offering an acceptable choice of fish was always a little difficult to arrange – not just because of weather and consequent price rises, but because there are so many kinds of fish it is impossible to stock all of them all of the time. So someone is bound to be disappointed.

My favourite remaining image from the shop is of the man who walked in one day carrying an open cookery book, over the top of which he peered in order to say, "Monkfish please." Alas, we had none. I started to say coaxingly, "But we do have some nice . . ."

Only he had gone by then.

You need a bit of forgiveness in you, buying fish. A willingness to compromise.

John's idea of compromise was to point decisively at the best and most expensive fish on show: a wonderful, two-pound Dover sole which shone with life (even though it was dead). It was, he said, by far the nicest fish there, not just for quality but for size – a good, meaty beast. I should argue?

We took our purchase and sped homewards towards a wonderful meal.

There are many ways of dealing with a large Dover sole, and we will outline some at the end of

this chapter, but John's overwhelming preference was that he should cook this one whole – on the bone. In fact, he always prefers to cook large Dovers whole.

He said, "Of course, there will be occasions when you will need to fillet a sole – for instance, you may want to serve it with three or four different kinds of fish, in which case I would perhaps roll up the fillets with a stuffing. Or you may be looking for ways to spread one big fish into portions. There are always arguments for the other side, but I start from the position in which I really would rather not fillet – not with Dover sole, or, say, turbot." Why? "Because the flavour on the bone is better, it keeps its moisture and it wastes less."

A problem this raises, of course, is that it may be difficult to make a stock if you do not fillet your fish: John avoided the problem by using the head and skin; alternatively, as he pointed out, you can boil up sole bones *after* you have cooked the creature whole.

Another point worth thinking about is the simple question of price.

As I write, a good Dover sole will cost anything from £3.50 a pound to £5.50, which is a lot of money. I would actually get embarrassed, selling the creatures, putting one on the scales and informing the customer that this little number would cost them perhaps £8.

One day, though, I went out on a fishing boat, watching the men haul in the trammel nets which trap sole and other fish on the bottom of the sea bed. It is a tiring job which goes on for hour upon hour on a slippery deck which goes up and down in a very queasy fashion. Every so often they pause to smash crabs which become entangled in the netting, then they pull out another sole and on they go.

The man I spoke to had been doing this for sixty-three days in a row, without a break. I didn't feel so rotten about the price after that.

But what do you get for your money?

John's view is that the reputation of the Dover

sole is certainly well-deserved. "I used never to cook it," he said. "But there were some days when there was nothing except Dovers and I cooked one and thought, God, it's marvellous, isn't it?

"It's very firm, a very meaty texture – and the flavour is fine. I think when you get a big dover it deserves its reputation. But the small ones I don't think are worth it – the flavour is not as good and there is an awful lot of bone to fish."

How, though, was he going to approach the one we now had on the restaurant table?

Picking it up, putting it down, looking every inch like a man about to talk to himself, John said he would cook it whole, yes, or rather take the head off, make a wonderful cream sauce, no a sage sauce with onion and . . . raspberries? Why not a raspberry and cream sauce? No, why not with some sage too, why not . . .

On and on.

I was relieved when he finally picked up a cloth and a knife and set about skinning the fish. At least it was a start.

BASIC PREPARATION

As there are two ways of skinning a Dover sole it is probably inevitable that John should prefer one of them and I the other.

To be democratic he took the top skin off his way and the bottom using mine. Each of us still prefers our own method but here are the options for you to judge: (do remember, by the way, that the top skin is totally inedible and the bottom white skin can only be eaten if you scrape off all the scales).

Cut a shallow line in the skin right across the fish, just under the head, using the gutting hole as a starting point.

Now scrape away at the flesh with the point of the knife until you have peeled back a large enough flap of skin only to grab hold of with a cloth. Cut a little way down the side of the fish where the roe makes the flesh feel "flabby". Pull the skin back and pare off any flesh as soon as it starts to come off with the skin. In fact, one or two quick hard

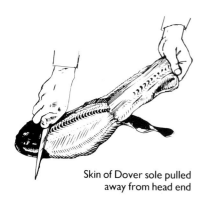

Skin of Dover sole pulled away from head end

tugs should do the job.

Now for the second method:

Turn the fish round and start at the bottom end. Slice across the tail quite hard with a knife and, keeping the blade at right-angles to the fish, scrape upwards an inch or so, four or five times.

A flap of clean skin will rise up, which you then grab hold of and pull. If the flesh sticks, cut it away from the skin with the knife-point; if it doesn't, just pull hard and be careful no one is standing behind you or they will get a slap in the face with a wet sole skin.

Whichever way you choose to do this job, remember that there is always a third option: ask the fellow who sells you the fish to do it.

John, with his Dover sole gleaming skinless before him, now cut off its head, trimmed the side fins using a pair of scissors and flicked out the small amount of congealed blood sticking around the top of the backbone. Finally, he prised out the pink roe, for use in the stock.

To make that stock he put about a pint of water into a saucepan and threw in all the fish trimmings including the skin, plus one and a half finely chopped onions, a handful of chopped celery tops and one crushed garlic clove (sliced before crushing, to ease out all the flavour).

He put this on to boil while he gently melted an ounce or so of butter in a long, flat baking tin; when it was ready he flopped both sides of the fish in it, twisted on a little black pepper and put the fish in the oven, uncovered, to bake. The gas was set at Gas Mark 5 (375°F, 190°C). It was to cook for twenty minutes.

John now returned to the question of what sauce to make. He said, "Yes, I think it will definitely be a sage and raspberry sauce. I think the colour will look fantastic and —"

Someone in the kitchen cut in, "Sole with *raspberry* purée . . .? Oh come on . . ."

John's smile went a bit fixed. I asked if he did indeed have any reservations about using raspberries with fish and he said, "No." Then,

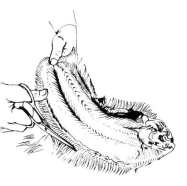

Trimming side fins from skinned Dover sole: cutting up from tail end is better. From head fins fold back and snip away with scissors

"The only reservations I have are that I haven't done it before." And finally, "But my hunch is that it will be quite good."

So we all felt tremendously confident, though possibly one or two of us laid mental plans for a late meal of Marmite sandwiches.

John meanwhile chopped the remaining half onion into minute pieces, thrusting his fingers to the edge he was cutting as a guide for the knife: that way he achieved really thin slices and his own fingernails protected his flesh from the blade. He cut the pieces lengthways and then across, then added the onion to a one-ounce piece of butter melting in a small saucepan on a low heat.

Pausing to set some new potatoes to boil, John then chopped the stalks from six fresh sage leaves. The stalks went into the boiling stock, but the leaves were carefully piled one on top of the other and put by for use right at the end.

When the onion had cooked for about six or seven minutes he spooned a small amount of stock into this pan and took it off the gas.

In went the controversial raspberries. A wooden spoon stirred and mashed the lot and the resultant pink mess was tipped into a sieve over a bowl. A spoon and spatula were used to crush out every bit of liquid and scrape into the bowl all the mush which accumulated on the underside of the sieve.

"May I taste that?" I asked politely.

"No."

Oh.

But then he left the room for a moment and I treated myself to a sneaky lick. It tasted like raspberry and onion. Visions of a Marmite sandwich arose once more.

Returning, John strained the stock and moaned, "As ever, I've added too much water to this, so there is some reduction to do . . . tastes good, though . . ."

Though sometimes sensitive to attempts by outsiders to taste his cooking while it is in progress, John does so himself all the time – more often than I care to make a note of, in fact. It is a

continual process which he recommends for every cook: constant tests and minute adjustments to taste – more butter, more pepper, whatever he feels is necessary. It is a personal judgment and explains why he is sometimes reluctant to say *precisely* how much of a particular ingredient should go into a dish. Some decisions, the cook can only make as the meal progresses.

Someone else came into the kitchen at this stage, heard what John was doing with the fish and raspberries and muttered something like "Good God". I tell you that so that you will understand the background of subtle tension which developed as John doggedly swept on with the meal.

What happened next may sound a little complicated but, as John pointed out later, the whole process could have been simplified if he had made the stock a little less watery in the first place.

Because it was too thin he poured a cupful of it into a saucepan together with half of the thick cream and began reducing it on a high gas.

Meanwhile the bulk of the stock was reduced on a separate ring, to be added in splashes to the sauce mix as the minutes passed. The only advantage of using two pans to reduce these mixtures was that it increased the surface area available for boiling, and therefore speeded things along.

After seven or so minutes of reduction, John added the raspberry and onion sauce to the stock and cream mixture – tasted it, then sprinkled in a small pinch of salt. On with the reduction.

It took a further five minutes to achieve the right balance of taste and consistency. On several occasions John added small extra splashes of thickened stock – he also poured in the last half of the cream. But finally he decided it was ready: "You need a syrupy, running sauce," John explained, testing by watching the liquid drop from a wooden spoon. "It must be able to cling to the roof of the mouth."

Now there were only two things left to do. John tested the Dover sole and found it

perfectly cooked after its twenty minutes in the oven. It was only *just* cooked – still very firm, still clinging very slightly to the bone, but white all through. If this point ever worries you, bear in mind two things when trying to decide if your baking fish is cooked: the first is that you must catch it before it turns dry and crisp on the outside; secondly, the best way to test the inside is to make a tiny incision with a knife at the top end – that is, the thickest part of the fish – cutting right to the bone: if it is still pink or will not easily come away from the bone, let it go on cooking. With larger fish such as brill and turbot, John will sometimes make a cut right down the backbone to speed up the cooking process if the outside is threatening to become dry.

His Dover sole was perfectly done, however, so he took it from the oven and poured the juice into the reducing sauce.

Secondly, he took the sage leaves which were still piled one on top of the other and gently rolled them into a tight little tube, which he sliced into eighth of an inch widths. The resulting rounds stayed more or less complete, and these he tossed into the sauce after it had come off the gas and had cooled for a moment or so.

He was ready to serve.

How would it be? We were agog.

Three of us gathered as John carved the cooked sole, effectively filleting it just as though it was raw. One long, thin half from each side of the fish was placed in the centre of a plate: the flesh held together like meat; there was no question of it breaking up, it was cooked so lightly.

Now the raspberry sauce was poured in giant puddles on each side of the fillet. The white of the fish was at once accentuated by the faint pink liquid dappled with green shreds of uncooked sage.

The pile of new potatoes was placed in the centre of the table and we took them, one at a time. (To have heaped whole portions into the sea of sauce would have spoiled the look of the food too soon.)

Several sage leaves piled up ready to be rolled – other longer leaves such as sorrel, spinach and mint can be treated in the same way

Sage leaves rolled ready for cutting

Rolled sage leaves cut into thin strips

We began eating.

I remembered a phrase about eating your own words but did not dare use it.

It was lovely.

The sauce was sharp, fresh but powerful – similar in style to the gooseberry sauce we had eaten with mackerel a couple of weeks previously but not as sweet, and much heavier. The sole had a delicious feel to it – a heavy texture which matched the power of the sauce. We were eating lunch but it was really too grand for that: it would have made a wonderful, regal dinner.

John gave us raspberries and cream to follow. Then a rather nice raspberry liqueur. Just possibly he was making some sort of point.

VARIATIONS

Of course, the first problem facing anyone wanting to try this dish is that raspberries have a very short summer season. So what do you do? Three possibilities:

The first is that you might only cook them in season – which John favours but I think is a shame. The dish matches any season, not just summer.

The second, then, is that you can use frozen raspberries.

And thirdly, you could look for alternative fruits. John suggests redcurrants, lemon, lime or orange ("Just the juice from the citrus fruits, and a tiny bit of zest or it will be too bitter," he warned).

If not fruit?

"There are all your boozes," said John. "Dry vermouth, even red wine – a Rhône or southern French job, they have a lot of fruit and body without being too expensive. A cheap claret. But you would have to use quite a lot – up to half a bottle added near the end, then reduced afterwards. Dry cider would work too."

Asparagus might work even better, he felt. Using the chopped hard stalks for boiling with the stock – and some lemon juice – and slicing the poached softer heads lengthways in two or four, and laying them on top of the whole Dover sole.

An alternative fish, John thought, might be the monkfish, which has the flesh of a meaty lobster.

Monkfish would be suitable, he thought, because the texture had been an important part of the meal, and firmness was a quality which both kinds of fish shared. Anyone trying the monkfish, John thought, should slice it into cutlets about half an inch thick; it would shrink a little with cooking.

But there are other ways of handling Dover sole than simply cooking it whole.

John said that he might have filleted the fish into four pieces, then poached the fillets in stock. Removing the fish he would have reduced the liquid, adding butter and lemon with a few sage slices at the end.

It was even possible, he said, to fold a sole fillet over a single sage leaf with butter, and poach it just like that – removing the leaf as you ate, making a very light lemon and sage sauce with the stock.

Or, forgetting sage, he could have sliced the Dover sole right across the fish into two-inch steaks – with both skins still in place. Then a lengthways cut down the centre of each steak could have formed a pouch in which to stuff a mixture of lightly cooked mussels, parsley and butter. The steaks could be baked for about fifteen minutes in a moderate oven.

Best of all, John thought, it would be worth investing in some oysters – steaming them open in half a minute, adding the juice to a lemon and stock sauce and arranging the oyster meat with baked or poached fillets or steaks. Three or four oysters per plate would be superb.

But back now to those wonderful raspberries. This in brief is what actually happened:

DOVER SOLE IN RASPBERRY AND SAGE SAUCE
Ingredients for 4

2 lb (900 g) Dover sole
butter
1 pint (570 ml) water
small quantity of celery or celery tops
2 small onions
1 clove garlic

4 oz (110 g) fresh raspberries
1/4 pint (150 ml) thick cream
6 fresh sage leaves
salt, pepper

1   Skin the fish on both sides, removing its head and fins, smear with butter and black pepper. Bake in moderate oven for about twenty minutes.

2   Make a stock from about a pint of water, the sole head, skin and trimmings, chopped celery tops and onions, plus chopped sage stalks and one crushed garlic clove. Boil.

3   Finely chop half an onion and heat gently in about an ounce of butter and a little pepper. After five or so minutes take off gas and add raspberries. Stir.

4   Crush this mix through a sieve into a bowl.

5   Reduce a little stock with half of the cream, keeping back some stock to add later for taste (reducing this extra stock if necessary).

6   After seven or eight minutes add raspberry and onion mix plus small pinch of salt if needed. Reduce further, adding more liquid as necessary.

7   Add liquor from baked Dover sole, plus rest of cream.

8   Pile sage leaves on top of each other, roll and thinly slice. Add to sauce after it has been removed from gas.

9   Fillet the cooked sole using sharp knife. Serve with sauce.

SWEET AND SOUR CATFISH

"What's in a name? That which we call a rose
By any other name would smell as sweet."
Romeo and Juliet, II, ii.

Shakespeare, on the other hand, was not trying to sell catfish to the British public.

The truth is that there is an awful lot in a name, particularly with a delicate and slightly whimsical subject like food. John and I therefore appreciate that calling this dish "Sweet and Sour Catfish" involves an element of risk.

If we were being desperately slick we might have chosen a different title. "Fish Surprise" might have done the trick; or something ethnic-sounding and mysterious like "Chinese Yum Yum". Anything to worm a way round the fact that what John used for the meal was . . . catfish.

Even the fish shop did not call it that. Following a practice I established when behind the counter the title given to this fish was "Scotch hake" – a name I stole from a wholesaler who told me that other mongers got away with that. So Scotch hake it was, and the reason was simple: calling this fish by its real name put people off.

I did try it. Put out a sign saying "Catfish". People said, "Eer . . . *cat*-fish . . ." and bought cod instead.

John and I are sticking to proper titles here because a book is a good place to dispense with fantasies. We would only ask you to keep in mind the truth: that it is a lovely fish and the meal John made was delightful. So please do not be put off by blunt – but realistic – names.

On the slab, this fish will be offered to you as pinkish white fillets – quite thick and chunky – sometimes eighteen inches or more in length. It is cut to size when you buy. It is landed in this country by the Icelandic boats, which means it is probably quite old by the time it reaches the shops because it has a long way to come – but don't worry: it lasts the distance very well.

The nearest comparison to catfish I can think of is ordinary cod fillet, but you will find that cat has a slightly sweeter taste and a closer, more elastic texture. Why did we buy it? Because it was an overcast, dull, chilly day, and John was keen to make a "reassuring" dish: "Something warm and Christmas puddingy", he said as we walked. "Fish isn't generally regarded as reassuring but this will be – solid yet subtle. I think it will also be a store-cupboard meal, using things you're likely to have in the house anyway without having to spend more time shopping."

In other words, *he* wanted to get home. And though John had never cooked catfish before he was ready to be persuaded that its firm texture could withstand his plans for poaching fillets in a sweet and sour sauce. The ten ounces or so which he then bought cost barely a pound: catfish, presumably because of its name, which reduces demand, is one of the cheaper fish.

In the restaurant, some moments were spent heaving from various cupboards the impressive list of other ingredients which appears at the end of this chapter. If you find that dauntingly long, a careful glance will prove that everything you need will almost certainly be in your own larder at this very moment.

BASIC PREPARATION

Onion
Raisins

Muscovado

Black
pepper

Currants

Garlic

Sherry vinegar

Allspice

Ginger

John Kenward with
larder ingredients
assembled for sweet and
sour sauce

Having assembled the produce, John began the meal by quickly slicing up one and a half medium-sized onions: fine slices fragmenting onto a chunk of butter in a small saucepan, which he set on a low gas.

This meal, he admitted as he worked, was not so much a brilliant Kenward original as a piece of borrowed history, because the central idea had been taken from a book of medieval recipes lent by a friend (actually the recipes of Richard II's cook).

It seemed an odd thing, for a professional cook to borrow ideas from other sources, but John snorted at that: "People who claim to be creative are talking a lot of balls," he said. "There is very little that can be described as purely original – we're all influenced by what goes on around us, what we see and hear. Obviously I read cookery books and colour supplements and see other people cook in other restaurants, and some or all of that may get used – directly or indirectly – or it may be rejected.

"The destructive thing is taking as your starting point the idea that you must come up with something 'original' and 'different' – that gets in the way of real originality . . ."

What was real originality?

John shrugged. "I apply a small set of principles, which is to buy what is good and cook it appropriately. That doesn't mean there is only one way of doing it or there is only one thing to buy. If you take this book as an example – I would like to think that people will have an early night and read it in bed, not just have it propped up in the kitchen covered in flour. And maybe the next day or the next month an idea will appeal and it won't necessarily be in relation to the same ingredients, maybe something else – and I hope that people will be encouraged to think 'that might work', and give it a whirl . . ."

As he was talking, he sliced and crushed half of one garlic clove and added it to the gently simmering onion. It seemed a good point to dispense with philosophy and return to cookery.

Taking a dozen allspice berries, John crushed

them to fragments with the flat of a knife and then began chopping them finely, together with six wafer-thin slices of fresh ginger. The point about crushing the allspice before cutting is simply that it stops the berries shooting off the table. Try it and see.

This fine mix of spice and ginger, now almost mince-like in texture, was scraped into the onion, which had been cooking for about five minutes or less. A further quarter of an hour of cooking time was now allowed, until the onion itself was starting to brown and catch on the bottom, at which point John poured in one dessertspoonful of sherry vinegar: "You could use cider vinegar or wine vinegar," he said, "but this has got so much more flavour."

He also carefully weighed out and then added to the pot the following dried fruit: two ounces of large and one ounce of small raisins ("I think the large ones have almost too much distinct flavour," observed John. "I don't want this to be fish-with-raisins, so I'm using some lesser-flavoured small ones as well.") Also, one ounce of currants.

Thrusting my face over the steaming pot at this stage I was rewarded with a whiplash smell of fruit and vinegar which took the lining from my nose. John said that I had no need to be alarmed, lunch would be fine. I snuffled a reply.

The gas was turned up high after the fruit had been added, and John poured in half a pint of water, together with a dozen twists of black pepper and – after tasting – a further dessertspoonful of sherry vinegar: "The sweetness has not come out of the dried fruit yet," John warned. "When it does it could overpower the sherry vinegar, which is why I've added another spoonful."

Finally, in went one ounce of muscovado sugar – a dark, unrefined product which John favours – once again, because of its powerful taste. Time and again this issue arises: buying carefully, selecting ingredients for their quality and power, never making do with products which might appear to be a more natural first choice but,

because of their mass-produced nature, yield less in flavour.

The danger is in assigning such careful shopping – buying the right vinegar, sugar, yoghurt, herbs, anything – to the professional's role alone; but John dismisses the idea that the "ordinary" shopper has neither the time nor the skill to follow suit.

"It's not really an awful lot of bother," he insisted. "Most supermarkets have really good stocks of everything nowadays, and something like a bottle of sherry vinegar will last for months if not years. There is an awful lot more choice of food available than some people will believe."

After the sugar had been stirred into the bubbling sauce mix the pot was allowed to simmer gently, on a lowered gas, for a further half an hour. This was to allow the fruit to swell, and the liquid to reduce – so, of course, the pan was left uncovered to let out the steam.

There was nothing else to do during this period except read *The Daily Telegraph* and watch John give the pot an occasional prod. Not an interesting time. The fish, naturally, was away in the fridge.

When the half-hour had passed we were left with a brown, treacly mix not unlike the stuff you put in pies at Christmas – but a little more runny. The fruit had indeed swollen into plump pellets, and the aroma had altered from searing pungency to a strong, sweet scent which filled the kitchen and galvanised the taste buds as John poured the liquid into a wide frying pan, tasted it, then stirred in just a little more butter.

With the gas on a low to medium heat, John took the fish from the fridge and cut it into pieces two to three inches long, murmuring as he did so that as he had never used this fish before it was really "quite exciting". These small fillets he carefully placed on top of the cooking sauce, then sprinkled each with a little black pepper, covered, and left them to poach for four or five minutes.

Now, with the fish half-cooked, John made a

new decision, causing him to rush back to a side table and return with a small clutch of parsley which he chopped madly for a minute before sprinkling the fine green rain over the fish. Why?

"Partly to give it a bit of fresh flavour," said John, "because it's all a bit heavy. But also for the colour."

With the saucepan lid back in place, he spent the next five minutes raising and lowering the lid like a signal flag, prodding the fish and worrying about how it was cooking. The truth was, as he had never cooked catfish before (imagine that on a restaurant menu) he was not certain how long it would take: hence the probing finger, feeling for resistance and stiffness of flesh.

In the end, the total cooking time was ten minutes. With that behind us, John declared the meal ready, rather in the style of someone cutting a tape and opening a bridge. But he had us fooled. For even as we gathered like wolves round the kitchen table John merely ladled the fish onto warming plates – and reduced the remaining sauce for a further minute with a little more butter.

"Oy", we said.

But now at last he poured the sauce around the fish, and as thick grey clouds massed above us, visible through a huge skylight, we began eating.

And it *was* a reassuring dish. It was also precisely right for a cold day: strong, steaming, filling. Taking spoonfuls of white fish with great helpings of delicious, warming sauce, we could imagine our medieval ancestors hugging such meals to themselves in lieu of central heating or an Aga. Did Richard II bolt down this food? Was such a piping dish laid before King Arthur? Did it mark the Round Table?

These issues and more we pondered by the spoonful.

However, a more mundane point worth thinking about is that those of us who had the thinner parts of the fish – from the tail end – found more sauce flavour absorbed into the flesh than those with chunky pieces. I wondered aloud

whether turning the fish over in the sauce during cooking might have merged the flavours a little more – but John ruled that out on visual grounds: browned fish in a brown sauce, he pointed out, would have looked pretty unappealing.

He did concede, though, that with the very thick pieces of fish it might be worth slicing the fillets laterally in half, producing thinner "sheets" for the sauce to work on.

But that was a fairly minor point. The best accolade I can record for this meal is that at least one person at the table used their fingers to mop up the very last traces of sauce from the edge of the plate. Oh, and John belched. A very Christmassy affair.

VARIATIONS

The first thing to say here is that John was delighted to "discover" this fish because it had qualities normally associated with much higher prices. "If it was like anything it had the firmness of turbot," he said. "Most fish you fillet and the flesh will be quite rough, even with brill. When you fillet turbot you find almost a second skin underneath – and this had as well. It's an intriguing fish."

Taking that smooth firmness as his starting point, John proposed firstly that he could equally well have used it for a barbecue meal. "Or, again for summer, it would be very pleasant just baked or grilled with a little butter and pepper and served without a sauce – just a stir-fry of carrot and courgette."

For more wintry days he felt a good method would be to buy chunky, thick ends of the fish, cut into the flesh and tuck in wafer-thin slices of fresh ginger; then smear with butter and bake for fifteen to twenty minutes.

But if you wanted to stay with the idea of a strong sweet and sour sauce, a different way to achieve this would be with a simple tomato and onion mix.

"If you choose that way," said John, "you must either peel the tomatoes or you will have to sieve the mix, because you don't want peel in the

sauce – it just sticks to the roof of your mouth.

"So firstly you would blanch and peel the tomatoes or hold them over a gas flame and peel. Then you would fry some chopped onion and garlic in oil or butter, then add the tomatoes, sugar and vinegar and some water if necessary – it would depend on how much water came out of the tomatoes. Next you reduce the sauce in the same way, then add some fresh fennel or marjoram towards the end."

Apple could be used in the same way, he added, but in that case it would be better to use a little lemon instead of sherry vinegar (which would be too strong). Cider vinegar, however, should blend well with the apples – and Cox's would be the best fruit to use: "More flavour."

On a more ordinary day it would be worth cooking catfish in a simple parsley sauce, John thought, using fish stock and onion as the base and adding chopped parsley right at the end. He would even use flour in this sauce if the day was cold enough to demand a bit more comforting bulk in the meal.

Or, keeping the sweet and sour mix exactly as produced this time, John would have happily substituted lemon sole fillets for catfish – though they would have to be skinned first and would certainly have required less cooking. Even cod fillets would make a pleasant sweet and sour dish, but small fillets only as the large would break up while poaching.

It is worth adding a final word about fish names. Just as fish recognise no boundaries as they drift from coast to coast, so Man seems to apply few verbal certainties to those varieties he likes to eat. What is coley to the English is saithe to the Scottish; what is red fish to one fishmonger is red bream to another; mock halibut here is Greenland halibut over there. Buying "prawns" from Scotland once I was amazed to discover scampi in the box which arrived next day, but that is how the animal is known up there. And so on.

Catfish, as I have pointed out, is my Scotch hake – yet just to add a little more spice of

confusion it is also known as wolf-fish (from the French *poisson-loup*) and rock turbot, and I have heard it called rock salmon, in my shop – which is also another name for huss or dogfish. Followed it all so far?

Well, Jane Grigson, in her book *Fish Cookery* points out that another French name for catfish is *loup de mer*: the same name, of course, as bass is known by. It's endless, you see.

So mind what you are buying, and if in doubt remember the pinky-white flesh and the shine like a second skin. And good luck.

SWEET AND SOUR CATFISH
Ingredients for 4

1½ lb (700 g) catfish (alias Scotch hake, rock turbot)

1½ medium onions

half garlic clove

12 allspice berries

6 fine slices fresh ginger

2 dessertspoons sherry vinegar (or wine or cider vinegar)

2 oz (50 g) large raisins

1 oz (25 g) small raisins

1 oz (25 g) currants

½ pint (275 ml) water or fish stock

1 oz (25 g) brown sugar

chopped parsley

black pepper, salt, butter.

1   Keep fish in fridge till ready to add to sauce.

2   Finely slice the onion and simmer in butter. Add half a crushed garlic clove.

3   Crush and chop allspice berries with fresh ginger – add to onion. Cook for about fifteen minutes.

4   Add one dessertspoonful of sherry vinegar, plus the dried fruit. Raise gas and add half a pint of water plus a dozen twists of black pepper. Taste,

and add one more dessertspoon of vinegar as necessary. Remember, the fruit has yet to add sweetness to the sauce, so the vinegar taste should be quite strong as this stage. Add salt if needed.

5   Add the brown sugar. Stir. Reduce for about half an hour. Add a knob more butter. Pour into a wide pan.

6   Cut fish into three-inch slices, place on top of sauce, sprinkle with black pepper, cover and cook gently for four or five minutes.

7   Add a little chopped parsley to each fillet and cover again. Test regularly with knife or finger and when fish is just cooked (about ten minutes) remove the fillets and keep warm.

8   Reduce sauce for a further minute with one more knob of butter. Serve.

9

SQUID IN ORANGE SAUCE

LEMON SOLE WITH SMOKED SALMON

MONKFISH MARINADE

The telephone rang mid-morning one day, and an excited voice on the other end of the line said, "I've got some squid!"

It was John Kenward, pleased as punch with his latest purchase of fish, crashing into the day with an invitation to start work right then and there. Didn't he know, I asked myself, that he was talking to Pre-Elevenses Man?

Being enthusiastic about squid is one of those things you find difficult to do before coffee. I don't know why. Perhaps because squid is such an ugly brute, protected from the world not just by its suckered tentacles and streamlined body, but by the very fact that it does not look tasty at all. No silvery sheen, no mottled hue, no sumptuous feel: just a long tube-like body with flaps on, and a sense of living rubber under the fingers.

We British usually react oddly to it. It is all right on holiday round the Mediterranean after the

first pint of red wine – but in England mid-week it usually runs a poor second to sausages – or tripe and onions for that matter.

But what could I reply to John Kenward? Fish being so unreliable it is wise to take opportunities for meals as they arise, and John had been engaged on a fruitless squid-search for some weeks now. Spotting a batch on the fishmonger's slab he had grabbed his chance, bought some, called me . . . and I said Okay, yes, great John, I'll come at once.

So began a meal which was not only lovely to eat, but was visually the most attractive of this series. It is ironic, really: something to bear in mind when summoning up the spirit to buy your own squid – that it may be ugly, but it can make the prettiest food.

When I got to the restaurant I found that John's enthusiasm had also run to a medium-sized lemon sole and a small piece of monkfish (there, another ugly one – though its head in this country is lopped off before landing, thus reducing the weight of the fish by a third). The sun was shining, John pointed out, and it was a great day to produce a plate of attractive cold fish delicacies.

Yes, yes, I muttered, let's just get on shall we . . .?

And he began work at once.

You should know first of all that, although they were made to complement each other, the three parts of this meal were quite separate and would make fine individual dishes. Also, we allowed them to grow cold, but they do taste just as pleasant eaten hot.

My advice would be to try each dish by itself at first, and then put them together when your confidence is strong. It is only when they are presented as a combined group that the beauty of the dish really becomes apparent, but you can afford to wait for that advantage.

So, although John did his cooking all at once, with several things happening at any moment, I am setting them out here as separate sections.

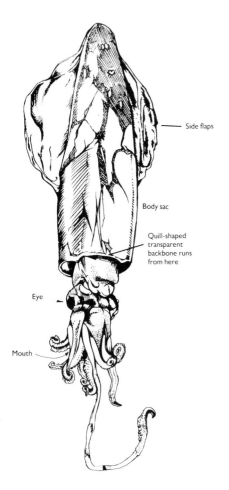

Side flaps

Body sac

Quill-shaped
transparent
backbone runs
from here

Eye

Mouth

Squid: the main parts

THE SQUID: The most comforting fact to consider when contemplating a squid is that, despite the exotic appearance, it is thoroughly British.

Customers in the fish shop often seem shocked but delighted to learn this truth. Having delivered their first salvo of disgust, they would stand open-mouthed on learning that the creatures they were attacking had been landed by Sussex fishermen on Sussex beaches (bear in mind that some of these squid measure two feet from tentacle tip to toe and look quite imposing draped over the trout and plaice). I found that patriotism often clinched a sale: customers could empathise better with a squid that was local.

There are foreign imports as well, of course – but the larger of these warm-water squid tend to be tougher than the natives and you should always try for the fresh local fish if it is available. As a last resort there is frozen calamari, the small American squid which many fishmongers stock as a matter of course. And at the time of writing I hear that huge quantities are being caught off the Falklands – but I have not tried them.

Whatever you buy, your first task will be to clean the brute – assuming that your friendly fishmonger has avoided doing this for you. It is in fact an easy, though slightly squirm-inducing job.

This is what John did with his twelve-ounce fish.

He laid the squid flat on a chopping-board, grabbed the head with one hand and the body with the other, and gently pulled . . .

Off came the head, and with it the entire workings of the poor squid's interior (John was careful not to squeeze the body too hard or the guts would have been trapped inside; if that does happen you must spoon them out with your fingers, subduing the impulse to cut open the body as the shape of this dish demands that it remains whole).

John now sliced off the head and threw away the guts of the fish. Then the main body had to be separated from its clear plastic-like backbone or

Head, tentacles and gut
pulled out of squid body
sac

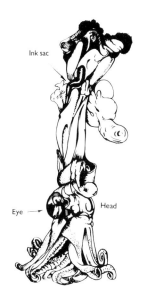

Head, tentacles and gut
separated from squid
body sac – guts thrown
away. Silvery coloured
ink sac can be kept and
used to make black sauce

Squid body squeezed
concertina-like to eject
the end of the backbone

Pulling backbone from
squid body sac

quill, a move which John carried out quite simply
by grasping the body with a cloth (to prevent
slipping) and pushing top and bottom into a
concertina-shape; up popped the tip of the
backbone, sprouting from the top of the fish like a
cellophane tree, which John pinched between
finger and thumb and pulled out.

An alternative method is to lay the squid body
on the chopping-board, find the top of the
backbone with a knife blade and pinch downwards
while withdrawing the body. The bone should then
stay under your knife.

The head and tentacles, and the body itself,
John placed in a medium-sized saucepan with
about one pint of cold water, together with half a
crushed garlic clove, half a sliced onion, six twists
of black pepper and some chopped parsley stalks.
If your squid is too long for the pan, simply cut it in
half.

The pot was set to boil while John added four
or five allspice berries, which he crushed finely
with the flat of a knife, the juice of half an orange,
and one teaspoon of sherry vinegar (wine vinegar
will do, though there is less taste so you may want
to use a little more).

Now the whole mix was stirred then covered.
John explained, "We are going to be frying the
squid in rings, but I'm boiling it first to make it
tender. With the very small squid that mightn't be
necessary, but I suspect that the larger ones have
more flavour anyway."

Could the fish simply be boiled in plain water?

"It could, but this is better because the flavour
gets right into the flesh while it stews – and then
the stock will be the basis of the sauce I'm going to
make."

The pot was allowed to boil for twenty-five
minutes – a time which John used to prepare other
parts of the meal, which I will describe later – after
which the squid's eight-inch body was pink and
swollen and soft, but not quite cooked.

"Now I'll just cool it under cold water," said
John, scooping body and head from the steaming
pot, "so that I can give it a proper clean . . ."

Mouth of cooked squid
pushed up and out of
head

Cooked squid body
sliced into rings

Be warned that this is where things become rather richly basic.

Taking the squid head in one hand, John used his fingers to prise out the eyes – yes, yes I know how that sounds but it is the work of moments; stay calm. Next, he squeezed the head so that the centre of the unsevered end bulged outwards, revealing the hard black beak with which the live squid gets its own back on the rest of the world. Again, using his fingers, John plucked out this beak and threw it, together with the eyes (are you still with me and conscious?) into the stock pan.

Now he poked around inside the tube to make sure it was totally clean, after which he picked off the pinkish outside skin, leaving a smooth, flawless surface – like rubber. From this body he cut the side "wings", two-inch long flaps – which he sliced in half lengthways, and put by.

The head he also halved lengthways (it looks better than in chopped pieces) and finally he sliced the tube-like body into rings a quarter of an inch wide.

With the fish now ready for its final cooking, John turned to the business of making a sauce.

Firstly, he chopped up three or four heads of fresh parsley, ready for using right at the end. Then he peeled another small onion and began to cut it, saying, "Unusually, I'm slicing this into rings instead of ordinary slices because it will add to the . . ." he hesitated, then went on with the over-emphasis of someone who has caught himself at an unexpected phrase, ". . . textural and visual delights."

What he meant was that the onion rings would look nice with the squid rings.

John now added a generous knob of butter and a little olive oil to a heavy frying pan, plus three or four twists of black pepper, and set it on a high gas. When the pan was sizzling hot and able to withstand the cooling effect of the fish, John tossed in the squid pieces, pointing out as his hands flicked away from the spitting fat that it wasn't the sort of dish children gathered round to watch cooking. Take note, do.

After two minutes, John added the onion rings, and throughout the five minutes total cooking time he prodded and tossed the food so that it could not stick or burn. For the last fifteen seconds he threw in the chopped parsley, turned it rapidly, then spooned out the food onto a plate, saying, "There's just the sauce to make now."

Using the same frying pan with its wonderful-smelling residue of oil and butter and parsley, John poured in four dessertspoonfuls of stock from the liquid used for boiling the squid, plus another knob of butter and the juice of quarter of a lemon. ("It's more acid than orange and I need that for de-glazing," said John.)

With the pan on medium heat he scraped the sides and bottom with a spatula, mingling the concentrated solids with the rest of the liquid, reducing for a minute or two then removing from the gas. Now ready, he poured the sauce over the waiting squid.

At this point I tried a single ring – lured by an aroma which had filled the kitchen. Not rubbery, not chewy . . . just firm with the texture of barely cooked pasta, and a marvellous heavy, rich taste which clung to the mouth and tongue. I would cheerfully have wolfed the rest but John wanted the squid to be part of a grander design so he set it to one side and warned me off while he got on with the rest of the food.

It suddenly occurred to me that just an hour before I had been yearning for elevenses and peace. An hour is a long time in cookery.

LEMON SOLE: This part of the meal is much easier to prepare, but potentially quite wasteful because it uses a very small amount of smoked salmon – which you may find awkward to buy. If you have a handy shop which actually slices smoked salmon from a side you are in luck, for you can buy exactly what you need: barely more than a single ounce for four people. But if you can only find the pre-packed fish you are going to be stuck with anything from one to three ounces too much: in which case it is your sad sacrifice to pig the rest

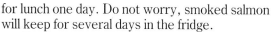

for lunch one day. Do not worry, smoked salmon will keep for several days in the fridge.

John's first act was to fillet the lemon sole into four parts (see pp 14 and 15) by quarter-cutting them down the backbone. Next, he skinned the fillets, putting away the skin and bones because this time there would be no need for stock or sauce (he could use them for another dish later in the day). Finally, he halved the thickness of each fillet by making a very careful horizontal slice along each. "It rolls better when it's thinner and these are quite fat fillets," John explained.

A word of warning here. When I tried this technique some days later – admittedly with plaice rather than the firmer lemon sole – I found it quite difficult to achieve a straight line and ended up with several interestingly shaped but useless bits of fish instead of a neat top and bottom. Make sure you have a steady hand and a very sharp knife when you try it – and be prepared to conjure up instant recipes for fish fragments if you muck it up.

Skinned quarter fillet of lemon sole sliced horizontally – only necessary for large thick fillets which can then be rolled more easily

John, however, was careful enough to end up with perfect fillets, to each of which he added a twist of black pepper and a thick finger-smeared layer of butter.

Now he chopped up four or five heads of fresh parsley and murmuring "a symphony of parsley" spread the bright green fragments over the butter. On top of this he placed a fine strip of smoked salmon, just a little narrower than the lemon sole fillet.

Finally, starting with the thick end, he made a firm roll of each piece of fish.

To cook it, he used the same, unwashed pan in which the squid had been fried, adding a quarter of an inch of water, setting the pan on a low heat, and covering with a saucepan lid.

Fillet of lemon sole rolled from wide end with smoked salmon filling

It took about six minutes. John, as always, prodded the rolls to see if they were ready, saying, "It must be firm but springy – it goes back to its shape after you've pressed it, but it isn't hard."

The important thing is not to overcook these rolls or they will break up at the next stage: after

chilling them thoroughly in a fridge to make them bind, John cut fine rings from each roll, perfect disks of white and orange and green. Saturn itself never looked so good.

MONKFISH: This part really is terribly easy.

John first sliced the remnant of bone from the gelatinous white flesh of his small chunk of monkfish, then poached the meat, half-submerging it in fish stock with a lid on the pan. It took fifteen minutes to cook, and if you have no stock, the usual mix of water, chopped onion, parsley and garlic will do, plus a little lemon juice.

When the fish was cooked (do remember that monkfish shrinks on cooking; it can be important when you are considering portion sizes) John cut it into quarter-inch thick slices, each about the size of a tenpenny piece. While these were cooling he splashed four teaspoonfuls of olive oil into a small dish, together with three florets of chopped parsley and a small squeeze of fresh lemon.

Into this mixture he carefully placed the pieces of monkfish so that each was touching the marinade. They were still a little warm when they went in, but this did not matter. The fish stayed in the marinade for half an hour, during which time John turned the pieces over just once.

Now they were ready to eat.

Setting out the food, John was able to take a little more time than usual over the arrangement because it was a cold meal and delays were not important. He used white plates and started with the squid – a collection of brown rings with the flare of head and tentacles on two of the plates, with a small spread of sauce in a surrounding splash.

Next, he arranged the slices of lemon sole, overlapping but placed so that the colour contrasts were clearly visible, and placed well clear of the squid and its sauce.

The medallions of monkfish were also given space of their own. The marinade in which they had been lying was poured on top. And finally, a very thin strip of smoked salmon was laid on the plate to add a little more colour and shape.

It was a pretty dish, but it did not give the impression of fussiness or of hours spent with tweezers and a microscope: the emphasis was on arrangement and not construction.

My favourite part was the lemon sole, mainly because of the undercurrent of smoked salmon which came through a few moments after biting into the white fish. The squid was as lovely cold as it was hot; and the monkfish, with its gentle lemon and parsley marinade provided a good fresh contrast to the squid strength. A little more of each would have made a wonderful full meal, with a side dish of crisp vegetables or salad in summer. As a simple collection of starters it was stunningly appealing.

VARIATIONS

SQUID: When considering other ways of using squid the first question to overcome is, why bother? After all, it is odd to look at, requires a robust attitude in handling: is squid really worth the effort?

John is clear on the point. "Everyone's first response is that squid is rubbery, which is rather what I used to think," he said. "But that is only because I had it when it had been cooked poorly.

"Squid has a curious and interesting texture – very like cheese, or a block of something. It's not like any other meat, and it's quite wrong to think of it as tasteless, as some people do.

"It has a very good taste. It responds to cooking in much the same way as scallops – very, very similar. Cooked very hot, fried, scallops and squid develop this wonderful rich flavour and smell, similar to baking or frying lobster. It is a marvellous rich taste, not like fish at all – not like anything else at all."

So what would he propose as an alternative method of cooking squid?

John's first response was to suggest a simple change from onion to spring onion – chopped lengthways in quarters or halves and fried with the squid rings very briefly – in all other respects keeping to the original recipe. Besides adding a variation of taste this method gave more colour to

the dish.

More exotically, he suggested stuffing squid tubes with a terrine mix.

"Boil the squid in the same stock – or water with lemon, garlic and onion – then cut the body into two-inch tubes," said John. "Chop up the unused fish and fry it, adding some chopped onion, tomato, garlic with marjoram or thyme or parsley. After you've fried it, allow the mix to cool then put it through a food processor with one or two egg yolks – but not cream because it doesn't want to be too runny.

"Then take the mix and stuff the squid tubes and bake them hot for ten minutes."

If it was too runny to stay in the tubes?

"A bed of tinfoil curled up at the ends could seal the tubes," said John. "Or to avoid the problem altogether some boiled rice could be used as a binder instead of egg yolk."

Of course, if you are short of time or patience, there are simpler ways of dealing with this fish. Playing around one day with a free squid given to me after a trip on a Sussex trawler I simply threw away the head and guts, cut the body into long thin spaghetti-like strips and boiled these in a basic stock mix. Then I fried them very quickly with some onion rings in a mix of olive oil and fresh lemon juice with a little salt and pepper. The memory lives with me still.

LEMON SOLE: "A paste-filling would work beautifully here too," said John. "Fillet, say, three lemon sole, splitting them to half thickness if they are large, and skinning them all. Then take half of one fish and make the terrine stuffing with it: you cook some finely chopped onion and garlic in a little butter, cool it, then add it to the food processor with the sliced half of fish, an egg yolk and some salt. Put a little too much salt in because the fish you will be rolling will absorb some of the flavour.

"Then spread the terrine mix in a thin layer over the fillets – spread it on the skinned side so you don't have flecks of skin on the outside of the

roll, and because the terrine flavour will merge with the fish better that way.

"Now roll it up from the thick end and bake it covered for about ten minutes in a medium oven."

Why cover it?

"Because the bits at the side of the roll might cook too quickly otherwise."

MONKFISH: There are almost limitless ways of marinading or dressing a firm white fish like the monk. John suggested three alternatives to the method he chose:

i Use the same ingredients as before – that is, olive oil, lemon juice and parsley – but add half a clove of finely chopped garlic as well, plus a little salt and pepper. The result will be a sharper, spicier taste which, if taken as a starter, may make you want to consider more carefully the strength of the main meal to follow.

ii Add some chopped tomato, basil, and garlic to a little olive oil with salt and pepper, then add the fish exactly as before.

iii Dress the poached medallions of monkfish with a little sour cream, chives and a point of thoroughly crushed garlic.

Or, if you want to eat the fish hot, John proposed cutting three-quarter-inch slices of monkfish and poaching them semi-submerged in a basic stock mix. "Only cook it for about three to four minutes," he said. "Or until it is cloudy on top. Thin slices will obviously cook much faster than a single lump.

"I wouldn't cover it during the poaching because generally with fish it can be tricky – because by covering you are allowing the top surface to cook and you can never be sure it is cooked in the middle. I covered the lemon sole because that type of fish was going to cook quickly."

When the monkfish is ready, take it out and add some butter to the cooking stock with more garlic if (after tasting) you feel it is necessary. Then reduce the mix vigorously and right at the end add some chopped parsley or chives.

"That adds some colour, because it is a very white fish," said John.

Finally, mix the fish and sauce and begin eating: but remember that John always tastes his sauces during preparation and just before serving. If you are not happy with the balance of taste, just alter it – more salt, lemon, pepper, whatever you feel is necessary to suit your preference.

But now we can return to square one, with a reminder of the three parts of the meal which John prepared.

SQUID IN ORANGE SAUCE

Ingredients as a starter or light meal for 4

1 × 1½-2 lb (700-900g) squid

1 pint (570 ml) water

½ clove garlic

2 medium onions

3-4 florets fresh parsley

4-5 allspice berries

½ orange

1 teaspoon sherry vinegar (or wine vinegar)

pepper, butter, olive oil

stock

lemon juice

1   Clean the squid by pulling off its head (which removes the guts) and pushing out the backbone. Use a cloth to prevent slipping.

2   Boil the head, tentacles and body in a pint of water with half a crushed garlic clove, half a sliced onion, six twists of black pepper, some chopped parsley stalks. If the squid body is too long for the pan, cut it in half.

3   Add four or five crushed allspice berries, the juice of half an orange and one teaspoon of sherry vinegar. Stir, cover and cook for about twenty-five minutes on a medium heat.

4	Remove fish and cool under water. Peel off skin, remove eyes and beak and lingering guts.
5	Slice head in half, lengthways. Cut off side flaps from body and also cut in half, lengthways.
6	Slice quarter-inch rings from squid tube.
7	Cut a medium onion into rings. Heat olive oil and butter with a little black pepper in thick frying pan.
8	When sizzling hot, add squid rings. Cook for two or three minutes while turning with spoon, then throw in the onion and cook for a further two minutes.
9	Add a little chopped parsley, turning rapidly and cooking for a few seconds. Remove fish from pan.
10	Add four dessertspoons of stock to the same pan, reduce and de-glaze with lemon juice and a knob of butter, scraping pan sides and bottom while heating.
11	Serve, or cool first.

LEMON SOLE WITH SMOKED SALMON

Ingredients as a starter or light meal for 4

2 medium lemon sole

1-2 oz (25-50 g) smoked salmon

3-4 florets fresh parsley

butter, black pepper

water for poaching

1	Fillet and skin the lemon soles, and, if necessary, halve the thickness of the fillets by slicing laterally. Smear on a layer of butter and a little black pepper.
2	Chop four or five parsley heads and spread onto the butter.
3	Add a fine strip of smoked salmon running almost the length of each fillet.
4	Roll the fillet, starting from the thick end.

5 Poach in frying pan with quarter-inch of water, covered, for about six minutes.

6 Remove fish, chill the rolls then slice finely with a very sharp knife. Serve.

MONKFISH MARINADE

Ingredients as a starter or light meal for 4

1-1 ½ lb (450-700 g) monkfish

fish stock for poaching

½ onion ⎫
    ⎬ to make stock if none available
½ garlic clove ⎭

4-5 teaspoons olive oil

3-4 florets fresh parsley

squeeze of lemon

1 Remove fish from bone and poach semi-submerged in fish stock, uncovered, for about fifteen minutes.

2 Take fish from pan, cut into small pieces. Add to a marinade of: four or five teaspoons of olive oil, three florets of chopped parsley and a squeeze of lemon.

3 Leave for at least half an hour, turning once. Serve and pour marinade over the monkfish.

10

MUSSEL AND GINGER SOUP

MOCK HALIBUT WITH TOMATO AND ONION SAUCE

This time I went shopping on my own, ploughing a lonely furrow through the crowded pavements of Lewes with the oddest brief of all . . . to surprise John; to buy something he would not recognise and had never cooked before.

Why? Because fish shops very often run out of things, and when that happens customers tend to go home with some strange beast they didn't want and have no idea how to cook. Pity the poor chap sent to buy trout, only to return lamely with grey mullet, dumping the package on the draining-board, waiting for expressions of joy from his wife – in vain. Cooking fish you have never tasted before can be a trying experience.

So it was agreed that I should do exactly this to John, test him with the unexpected and see what he could do.

The trouble is, of course, that trying to surprise a professional cook is not easy. Whatever fish you choose they are almost certain to have prepared it dozens of times before in batches of a hundred, or studied at college under a tutor specialising in exactly that species. "Oh, *that* old thing . . ." they will say.

Gloomily pondering the options, I made my way to the fish shop.

Down in Cliffe High Street there were a dozen or so varieties of fish on sale: some nice trout, a wonderful brill, some Dover soles, magnificent in their armour-plated coats, cod fillet of course . . .

Nothing here to scare a chef. At the counter they told me that if I could just hang on for a couple of hours there would be additional stocks up from London: yes, I replied, but by then our cook will have gone insane. At which point my eyes fell upon a little pile of mock halibut, and I knew that I was saved.

Mock halibut?

Like catfish (see page 84) it is landed in this country by the Icelandic boats, and also like catfish it has at least one alias – Greenland halibut being the most common. It appears as long, wide fillets, differing from the pure halibut in the fact that its skin is always dark: there is no white underside. It is not as firm, dry or fine-tasting as pure halibut either, but is still useful as a cheap, filling meal.

For me, its chief advantage on this day lay in the fact that it is not a "restaurant fish" – no matter how well-treated it would be the equivalent of haute-cuisine sausages on any menu. Therefore, John Kenward almost certainly would never have cooked it before.

I bought a little over a pound and, chuckling over my cunning, quit the shop – pausing only to buy a pound of fresh mussels because they looked quite lively.

But what happened when I got back to the restaurant?

John sniffed the mock halibut like a cat, prodded it, flopped it up and down as if it was a live fillet which only needed jogging to return to

full vigour, and said, "It's one of the Icelandic jobs . . ."

How my little face fell!

To complete my downfall, helper Christine swept by at that moment, asking whether or not that wasn't some kind of halibut we had there. John put two and two together and said, "Mock halibut, actually."

Oh.

I was left clutching to myself the compensatory fact that, though recognising the fish, he admitted never having tasted or cooked it before – so the planned test was still valid.

I asked what he thought of the raw fillet. John shrugged. "It looks firm," he said. "But it doesn't look very interesting, though that is often a mistaken judgment you can make with fish. Mind you, the skin is extremely uninteresting – you'd be quite hard pushed to think of anything more drab, so I'll have to take that off . . ."

He was quite right about that – something I ought to have noticed in the shop, but didn't. Mock halibut when very fresh has a good, dark, shiny skin – almost black – but the older it gets, the more grey and mottled the surface becomes. A quick glance at our fillet showed that on this occasion the Icelanders had taken perhaps rather longer than usual hauling the batch across to England. It was indeed, grey.

Yes, I said, so what did John propose the average person should do when facing such a dilemma: an uninteresting fish which might or might not taste pleasant?

John made excuses to bustle around his kitchen for a while, poking his nose into pots and pans, picking things up, putting them down. But he was not fooling me: I knew he was stalling for time.

Three minutes passed.

Everything stopped. We all looked at John, and he said "I'm going to bake it." Yes, and . . .?

He thought a little more and then went on, "I'll serve it with a sauce – something strong enough in its own right, not just an accompanying sauce.

Quite well-flavoured but not enough to obscure the fish if it turns out to have a particularly fine taste . . .

"I don't mean one of our lighter stock-based sauces with just the flavour of citrus – it will have a texture and character all of its own, without being strong like chutney . . ."

A Cure-All Sauce which eliminated risk. If the fish tasted wonderful then the sauce would not be so strong that it ruined the enjoyment; but if the fish was dull the sauce could be spooned onto the fork more lavishly to give each mouthful some life. It seemed a good idea, but how to achieve it?

While I was making notes, John had gone to the shelf and returned with a single, very large and very ripe tomato. Now he produced a couple of onions, frowning with thought as he did so, occasionally prodding the fish once more as if just making sure . . .

When he was ready, he announced that because I had bought mussels as well he would make two dishes using the mock halibut – "I'll do a soup with some of these mussels and the fish . . . and I'll bake some fillets and serve it in the sauce . . ."

He began work, and once again, I shall divide up the two dishes which resulted.

BASIC PREPARATION

MUSSEL AND GINGER SOUP: John's first act was to tidy up the fillet – something he would need to do for both dishes.

This was quickly done, because it simply meant taking off the skin and cutting away the thin, feathery fringe attached to the main body of meat round the sides of the fillet.

To get the skin off, John pressed a knife through the meat at the tail end of the fillet, forcing the blade hard against the skin and then along to the "head" end while keeping a firm hold of the tail. It came off like a mackintosh.

The strips of flabby fish attached to the sides of the main fillet he cut off with two sweeps of the knife. John said he did this "partly to give me a bit more for the stock and partly because I think the

sides might collapse in the cooking and won't look good on the plate."

Finally, he cut off the small grey area at the top of the fillet where the guts of the fish normally leave their mark. All these trimmings, plus the skin, he added to half a pint of cold water in a saucepan, which he set on a medium to high gas to boil. "I'm only using half a pint of water for the soup because that's where the mussels are going, and they will produce more liquid," John explained.

Meanwhile he peeled and finely cut up one medium onion, and sliced and crushed a single garlic clove. He cut a piece of fresh ginger about the size of a small broad bean from a root, and peeled it, keeping the thin, fine peelings for almost immediate use, but holding back the solid piece of ginger for later.

The onion, garlic and ginger peelings went into the pan with the fish trimmings, together with six twists of black pepper.

It was now John's dreary task to clean up the mussels before adding them to the saucepan. As we pointed out on page 24 it is often necessary to "beard" mussels before cooking them – that is, pull off the threads and hairs at the shell seam, by which the mussel attaches itself to rocks or North Sea oil platforms.

In fact, the mussels I had bought were a particularly messy lot (these things do vary, some of the cultivated mussels you can buy are beautifully clean); John set about them with grudging determination – rinsing them under the tap and then pulling at the threads. If you are tempted to avoid debearding mussels please be warned that this is not wise even if, as John was planning to do, you are throwing away the mussel cases and keeping only the meat. The beards go right through the seam and attach to the mussel itself – trying to pull them from the cooked meat is a difficult job ending, more often than not, with a Christmas cracker effect: half the meat in one hand, half in the other.

By the time John had finished the job, the soup

Beard being pulled from shell of mussel

base was boiling hard. In went the mussels. John hesitated, and said, "I shall put in some dry vermouth . . . no, I shall use dry cider. People don't necessarily have a bottle of dry vermouth in the house and cider is something you can buy a small quantity of quite cheaply – though you could use either here."

Into the mix he poured about an eighth of a pint of cider. The smell of this mixing with the tang of cooking mussels was wonderful. The pot was not covered, so the steam and aroma was allowed free rein to gallop round the kitchen and out into the empty restaurant beyond. Marvellous.

After three minutes, John took a spoon and began removing from the pot any mussel that had opened and was therefore cooked. Obviously the ones in closer contact with the boiling water were cooking quicker than the ones on top, so these came out first. The last mussel was removed exactly eleven minutes after they first went in. Tasting the remaining liquor, John said, "It's got quite a nice flavour – the combination of mussels and the fish seems to be quite good."

He turned down the gas but left the soup bubbling gently while he set about pulling the cooked mussels from their shells.

A word of warning: mussels hauled from soup take a lot of liquid with them, trapped in the half-shell. Be careful you keep this – and pour it back into the pan when you have finished.

Once John had completed his finger-searing task he put the mussels in a dish to keep for the very end, and then strained all the soup through a sieve. The result? "It looks very grubby," John admitted.

Indeed it did. A kind of grey-brown liquid which made you think of old bath water or silt.

We stared at it. Tried to imagine sitting down to a bowlful of the stuff. Couldn't.

"Do you want to do some clarifying?" John asked suddenly. "Shall we do that?"

Yes, I said, let's.

Now, if you have never done this before, take heart: it is a simple and effective operation – and,

in truth, John need not have done it, for mussels and other ingredients had still to be added to the soup, effectively hiding some of the grubbiness. But for a really perfect dish, do try this.

John separated one egg and very gently whisked the white for a few moments until it was bubbly and cloudy. Then he poured this into the slightly-cooled soup and *very* slowly brought it to the boil: "If it boils too quickly the egg will break up," John warned.

Watching the tiny white clumps of cooking albumen form gradually round solids suspended in the liquid was rather like observing a magical snowstorm, or the appearance of Biblical manna. It took about three to four minutes and was a peaceful and rather fascinating spectacle. And when no more appeared, it was done.

Now pouring this clarified mix through a cloth and sieve combined (trickling it down the side rather than letting the liquid hit the bottom of the sieve) John found that he had achieved a much clearer, much prettier soup, which he returned to a very gentle gas ring.

Reaching at last for the small piece of ginger which he had peeled earlier, he sliced it very thinly and added these pieces to the pile of waiting mussel meat. Next John took about six ounces of fish from the tail end of the skinned fillet of mock halibut and cut it into even slices about three inches long and a third of an inch wide: "I'm using the tail because it falls apart less at that end."

After tasting the clarified soup, John added to it another half of finely chopped garlic, saying that it still needed "a little more flavour; more oomph", then tasted again and squeezed in the juice of one half of a small lemon.

The soup was nearly ready, but even now John hesitated – then went to fetch a little fresh parsley.

Cutting off four florets, he chopped them finely and threw this in with the mussels and ginger, explaining that this was mainly done to add some colour contrast, but also to freshen the taste.

Finally, the gas under the soup was turned up high and the bowl of mussels, ginger and parsley was tipped in, together with the thin strips of mock halibut. The liquid boiled, and as soon as the fish turned cloudy (which took just over four minutes of boiling) John switched off the gas and declared the soup ready for eating.

We sat down to small white bowls crammed with orange mussels, slivers of white fish and speckles of green parsley, and in all truth it was possibly the most delicious soup I have ever tasted (and that includes the lovely tomato stuff I used to get when I was nine, upon which I sailed boats of white bread and in which I revelled).

The mixture of ginger and mussels was outstandingly successful, though the mock halibut itself could have been anything fishy – its function seemed to be as much to add body as it was to add any taste.

The soup was warm enough for winter, fresh enough for summer. If you attempt no other recipe in this book do, please, try this one, and remember with the first spoonful the spirit of experiment which produced it.

MOCK HALIBUT WITH TOMATO AND ONION SAUCE: For this half of the meal, John had just over three-quarters of a pound of mock halibut, plus a commitment to make a baking sauce that would cater for any nuance of fishy taste. Would it work?

As I waited to record the first sign of theoretical weakness, John took hold of a medium onion rather in the style of John Wayne reaching for a six-gun: deliberate and firm. High Noon at Kenwards, I wrote in my book (though it was really half-past eleven).

Off came the onion skin, out came the knife, slicing lengthways then across until the pieces were small and fine – at which John scooped them into a saucepan together with a very generous knob of butter and one sliced and crushed garlic clove. He lit a very gentle gas and then sliced the single, ripe tomato, saying, "I'm not going to skin

this because I'll be putting it all through a sieve later. It's a good, ripe tomato – it's worth holding onto ones you buy in a shop until they get like this: they're usually much harder and sharper when you first buy them." The tomato went in with the onion, plus six twists of black pepper and the whole mix was stirred and then left to cook very gently for half an hour.

In this pause, John made the soup dish just described. You may like to do the same – or do some yoga, or start that Open University course you've always been promising yourself. Just remember to give the pan a prod from time to time.

When eventually it was thoroughly cooked – "well melded" as John put it – the sauce was removed from the gas and poured into a sieve. Breaking off for a moment, John set the oven to pre-heat at Gas Mark 4 (350°F, 180°C). Now he returned to the sieve and began pushing the thick mixture through the wire into a bowl, using the back of a spoon, pressing and scraping very hard so that every molecule of liquid was forced from the ingredients. He also made sure that he scraped the outside of the sieve itself to capture the thickest residue which gathered there. He then tasted the sieved sauce and added a little more black pepper and a very small amount of salt.

Almost ready to consign the fish to the oven, John sliced the mock halibut into pieces about six inches by two inches. Then he poured the sauce into a small, shallow baking dish and placed the fish on top, with a little pepper and a tiny knob of butter on each. Into the oven.

It took fifteen minutes to cook – but these fillets were of medium thickness and you will need to prod and test yours to see if they are ready before or after this time.

John ladled out the food with great care, keeping the pure whiteness of the fillet tops clear of sauce so that they stood out more in the surround of gentle red.

He served it with some lightly cooked spinach (fried in butter with some pepper and garlic) and

when asked why spinach he turned mountaineer and muttered: "Because it was there."

The important question now facing us was: had the dish worked? Was the sauce right for the fish?

The truth was that we were all grateful for the fact that it *did* work. Grateful because the skin signs proved to be quite correct and the fish eaten on its own proved to have only the mildest of flavours, with a very light texture. Hence the sight of everybody in the kitchen hastily spooning red sauce onto every mouthful.

Taken this way it was delightful: but please do not let my description put you off mock halibut, which can have a far more positive taste than the sample we tried. Just take a look at the skin, and if it is more grey than dark you know it is getting on a bit and will have lost taste.

I am comforted in my own error by John's view that the purchase of wonderfully fresh fish is something worth aiming at but impossible to achieve all the time, thanks to weather and inevitable hesitations in the selling chain. It even happens that fish bought to eat one day turns up forgotten in the bottom of the fridge twenty-four or forty-eight hours later. At these lesser moments a good sauce can – and did – work wonders.

VARIATIONS

MOCK HALIBUT: At the end of it all, John was convinced that he had been right to bake this fish, mainly because it had proved to be of such light texture that anything rougher might have caused it to crumble. But he was pleased with the simple tomato and onion sauce and immediately saw a use for it throughout the white fish range, from cod, catfish (see page 84) and haddock to coley (saithe, as it is known in Scotland) and even something as fine as turbot, though at this point you would probably want to cut down a little on the quantity of sauce you make: a small amount would go a long way with turbot.

John also proposed two other ways of making a quick, distinctive sauce which would have the

same broad appeal as his first attempt.

1 *Red pepper sauce*: Finely chop the onion and garlic clove just as before, cook it gently in the butter but add sliced red peppers as well as the tomato. Sieve after half an hour and add salt and pepper as you see fit.

2 *Onion and courgette sauce*: Fry very gently in butter some slices of courgette, with chopped onion and garlic. Sieve after half an hour and spoon in a little mustard: "I would use a strong English mustard," said John, "although most of those mustards you get in a pot will do – two or three spoons stirred in towards the end, and then the whole lot baked with the fish."

Could you simply smear mustard straight onto the fillet?

"You could, but I tend not to because it doesn't look very smart. If you had lemon sole or similar filleted fish you could put a thin layer of mustard in the fillet then fold it over or roll it."

Rolling or folding, however, is not really to be recommended for mock halibut, which is more likely to disintegrate under pressure.

As a final point, you may at some time be offered mock or Greenland halibut in steak form, cut straight across the bone. The chances are that these will have been frozen (I was never able to buy them fresh), therefore if these things worry you, just check the point with whoever is selling them to you.

MUSSEL SOUP: John felt that the type of white fish used in this soup was far less important than the mussels and ginger – though small strips of lemon sole fillet would have held together better, and cod fillet might have provided a different taste. The parsley, on the other hand, *was* important: "Not just for the colour," said John, "it added another dimension to the soup."

He went on to discuss a number of possible alternatives to this general idea of mussel soup, but nothing drew enthusiasm from him until he introduced the possibility of substituting turbot and oysters for mock halibut and mussels. The

dish sounded so wonderful that I will set it out in detail:

TURBOT AND OYSTER SOUP AND BAKED TURBOT

4-6 oz (110-175 g) turbot fillet per person

water

parsley

crushed garlic

black pepper

chopped onion

fennel (if available)

oysters (allow 2 or 3 per person)

egg white

lemon juice

1 Fillet and skin a piece of turbot, and use the trimmings, bone and skin to make a stock – together with parsley stalks, crushed garlic, black pepper and a little chopped onion, with a small amount of fennel, if you have some.

2 Open the oysters by inserting a knife in the seam and twisting. Then scoop out the meat over a bowl so that you catch the juice: take out everything you find inside the oyster, it is all edible. You will almost certainly need to pick out of the bowl the bits of shell which break off as you twist the knife – do this with care or you will end up with an overly crunchy soup.

3 Sieve the cooked stock, then gently clarify it with an egg white and strain it once more, this time through a cloth.

4 Now bring the soup gently to the boil once more and add a squeeze of lemon juice.

5 Now add the oysters and their juice, plus a little chopped parsley and, if necessary, some salt and pepper, with possibly a little more lemon juice. Remove from the gas.

6 Eat this soup while the turbot is baking in the oven Gas Mark 4 (350°F, 180°C) with a little butter on top of the fillet. The turbot will take approximately fifteen minutes to cook, but this will depend on the thickness of the fillet and must be tested at intervals.

Finally, here in brief detail, are the two dishes John prepared on this day:

MUSSEL AND GINGER SOUP
Ingredients for 4

1 lb (450 g) mussels
6 oz (175 g) white fish
½-1 pint (275 ml) water
1 medium onion
1 ½ garlic cloves
small piece fresh ginger
black pepper
⅛ pint (75 ml) dry cider (or dry vermouth)
egg white
4-5 heads fresh parsley
½ lemon

1 Put the skin and trimmings from the fish into half a pint of water with one finely chopped onion and a sliced and crushed garlic clove.

2 Peel a small piece of fresh ginger (about the size of a broad bean) and throw the peelings into the stock pot, holding back the peeled piece.

3 Add about six twists of black pepper to the stock.

4 Clean and de-beard the mussels.

5 When stock is boiling throw in the mussels.

6 Add the dry cider.

7 After about three minutes begin removing the cooked mussels. Keep in a bowl to save juice.

8 Lower the heat, take out the mussels from shell.

9 Strain the soup then clarify it (if you like) using a whisked egg white, bringing the soup to boil very slowly then straining through a cloth.

10 Cut ginger into thin slices – add to mussel meat with a little chopped parsley.

11 Cut the white fish into very thin strips.

12 Add more finely chopped garlic and the juice of half a lemon to the soup – tasting first to see how necessary this is.

13 Boil the soup and throw in mussel meat, fish, ginger and chopped parsley. In three or four minutes, when fish turns cloudy, serve.

MOCK HALIBUT WITH TOMATO AND ONION SAUCE
Ingredients for 2

12 oz (350 g) mock halibut (or other white fish)
1 medium onion
butter
1 garlic clove
1 or 2 large ripe tomatoes
salt, black pepper

1 Gently heat one finely chopped onion in a knob of butter with one sliced and crushed garlic clove.

2 Add the sliced tomato. Cook for up to thirty minutes.

3 Strain hard through sieve. Pour this liquid into shallow baking dish and place on it the skinned, sliced fish fillets.

4 Bake in a pre-heated oven for about fifteen minutes at Gas Mark 4 (350°F, 180°C). Serve.

11

TROUT FILLETS IN CREAM AND CORIANDER

The supermarket bustled with cheerful Monday morning life, setting the tone for the week ahead. A little girl swung from the rail by the baskets and fell off; assistants with unbending smiles gave endless directions for dog food, nappies, bread; mothers with trolleys set up road blocks in every aisle while they pondered choices or wiped someone's nose.

And here, by the packeted and pre-priced section for fresh fish, stood John and I, living out our latest fantasy menu.

Let us (we had theorised earlier) imagine a rich cousin visiting late and unexpectedly. Yes, and imagine the fish shop is closed or say there just *isn't* one – so many towns are without nowadays, thanks to Cod Wars and the price of a tonne of diesel.

What would we do? We would simply dash to the local supermarket to see what could be done about the holes in the larder. So off we dashed, and here we were by the fish in Safeway with John peering worriedly through clear plastic wrappers at filleted and skinned objects which seemed alien to him, foreign. He wasn't used to buying fish this way.

"It's difficult to see," he complained. "And you can't feel the fish. And the shininess gets in the way . . ."

He picked up a stiff-sided pack and tilted it, watching the white fillet inside flop first one way and then the other.

"It's all filleted or headless," he went on. "So there are no eyes to give a clue to its condition. I suppose the whole intention of the shop is to ease the way for the customer so that decisions don't have to be made: 'Put your faith in us . . .' "

We moved uneasily to the frozen fish section, but the choice was no easier there. "What's this? A cod steak 'Made with cod fillet'. I don't know . . ." (swallowing a little heavily) ". . . it could be really good."

But he was not convinced. So we walked back to the fresh fish and looked again, more purposefully this time: cod, haddock, plaice fillets; here were sardines, salmon, trout fillets, herrings without heads . . .

John reached for a pack containing filleted trout, hesitated, then said, "They look the best of the better-looking fish. I'll do something with these."

And into the wire basket went the gleaming pack with the label saying £2.70 for just over three-quarters of a pound of filleted fish. That was the equivalent of about one and a half pounds of whole fish, which later proved enough for three helpings. John mooched away into the aisles containing vegetables which spilled loose and free and touchable, and at once he seemed more at ease.

Here, he pounced on a bunch of fresh coriander – "For a sauce," he mused. Next, some perfectly formed Bobby beans, in another cursed but convenient see-through pack; then, passing on, there was a half pint of single cream ("A *creamy* sauce . . .") and finally some fresh pasta: *paglia e fieno* – a kind of thin tagliatelli.

It seemed enough. We turned and headed for the check-out queues with their shining tills and numbered lights – only before we got there John ducked suddenly into the frozen fish aisle and returned to that oblong piece of compressed fish steak which claimed to have been made with cod

fillet. Slipping it into his basket he explained that this was as good a time as any to experiment with frozen fish. Quite right: many people have neither time, opportunity nor inclination to buy anything else but frozen. It would be interesting to see if today's recipe would suit both camps.

We paid and hurried back up the hill, not to the restaurant this time but to the kitchen of John's home – a converted stable block situated a few hundred yards away, nestling in the shadows cast by bigger and grander high street buildings.

There was no important reason for this change of scene, other than we felt like a break from routine; and perhaps because we wanted reassurance that the restaurant's facilities, or atmosphere, made no difference to the cooking process. (And it didn't.)

Tearing open the packet containing the trout fillets, John at last got his fingers on, and nose to, the fish inside. Heavens, he had been dying to do that. Now he paused, smiled, then said, "They're very good." Then, "I think I'll grill these rather than poach them – that brings out the flavour in the oilier fish, because of the higher temperatures. I'll need to do that if there's going to be a strong sauce . . . which there is . . ."

The frozen cod steak went into some water to thaw, unremarked upon.

Work began. And what happened next entirely justified the decision to take a day off from the restaurant kitchen. For in all the recipes that John had produced for this series, never had it been so clear that he *prepares* as much as possible before he cooks.

It became clear this time for one reason only – peace. There are fewer interruptions at home than there are in a working restaurant kitchen – yes, even with children crying, the telephone ringing, visitors calling, home still has the peaceful edge. That meant John had more time in which to show clearly how much he likes to get things ready before cooking begins. As he explained: "An awful lot of cooking is organisation. That's why some people go to pieces under pressure in

the kitchen, because they haven't prepared themselves. It's what they say to me in the restaurant: 'How do you know what people are going to eat?' I don't. It's just a matter of having stuff prepared. You need a moment's reflection before you start so that you can see what needs to be done and you can make the necessary preparations."

BASIC PREPARATION

In this case, those preparations were simple but important: John knew that the stock from which a sauce would be made would take the longest to cook, so his first move was to put half a pint of water on to boil.

There was a flare of gas and a dry clack as the pan touched the ring.

Then, because he knew he would be using the grill quite soon he gently warmed it up (unlike the hob, it is electric) and dropped about an ounce of butter into the grill pan to melt.

He also placed a pan of water on an unlit gas ring for cooking the pasta at the end, and put another empty pan on a ring – this, to fry some leeks which he had discovered ageing quietly in the vegetable rack and had decided at once to use with the pasta.

A point in favour of such preparation – apart from simply helping you to time various parts of the meal so that it all ends together and nothing spoils – is that it saves on emotional energy, and cuts down the room for muddle.

John's kitchen is like many I have visited, in that wide areas of carefully designed worktop space are given over to the storage of everyday jumble: mixers, coffee-grinders, books and those holiday souvenirs you can never decide where to put. There seems seldom enough space for a decent game of shove ha'penny on the gleaming melamine, let alone a nice area in which to spread your pots. In that case, organisation becomes all the more important.

John, with his stock-water heating and butter melting, was quickly getting on with the job.

He took three or four stalks of coriander and

cut off the dozen leaf-heads, slicing them once or twice then putting them to one side for using later. The stalks he chopped into half-inch lengths and threw them into the warming water, explaining as he did so, "Fresh coriander is a very strong flavour which is actually quite difficult to control. It can overpower a dish very easily, so I'll have to be careful."

It would be a minimal vegetable stock, he said. Here was some fresh ginger – two thin slices went into the water. Now a crushed and sliced garlic clove. Three twists of black pepper.

The water was boiling, but he had more to add.

The two freshly discovered leeks had a disappointment to unleash in that they were going to seed – their centres had turned hard and fibrous. John sliced lengthways down the side of each plant and drew out these wood-like cores, chopping them and adding them to the stock together with the leek end-trimmings ("If you're not using leeks in the meal, put onion in the stock," he said.) Then he sliced the ends from the green Bobby beans, so that they were ready to use too.

Finally, a little seasalt went into the stock. That was unusual, because John normally waits to the end before touching salt, and asked why he had reversed the order this time he said he didn't know why, he just felt like it. Was it because there were no fish bones in there from which a salty taste might emerge? "Mm," said John, "that too."

Now slicing the leeks into thin diagonals he grew more forthcoming: "I know what I'm going to do," he announced. "I'm going to cook these leeks quickly beforehand in olive oil, rather than toss them in with the pasta to cook. This way they'll be ready together . . ."

A point of garlic was crushed and thrown into the pan waiting empty on the cooker. A spoonful of olive oil, and the gas was lit and turned up high. A sprinkling of salt, and as the pan began to sizzle, exuding that deep, rich aroma of hot olive oil, in went the sliced leeks – now tossed with stir-fry

energy for just two minutes, after which they
were turned into a waiting dish. Straight away, a
pint of water was poured into this leek saucepan
and replaced on the hob to heat up later. This
would be for the beans, said John. And no, it
wasn't necessary to wash the saucepan first, why
should it be? Sloth-like, I said I didn't know.

A splutter from the grill showed that the
butter warming there had liquefied. John now
turned the heat to medium, and wiped both sides
of the blood-rich fillets of trout in the spread of
butter, sprinkled a brief twist of black pepper onto
each, and thrust the tray back under the grill. As
an afterthought he also added that swiftly
defrosted lump of cod steak: it stood out under
there; oblong food always does.

By now the stock had been boiling furiously
for about fifteen minutes and the goodness had
leached from the vegetables into the liquid – which
John strained, tasted, added more salt and pepper
to, and then returned to a high gas to reduce and
thicken. He turned on the gas under the bean pan
and the pasta pan too. The sense of organisation
was becoming almost inhuman. When the
telephone interrupted the flow I was glad.

Yet it was only a momentary respite from
dogged progress, for now eight minutes had
passed since the trout fillets had been thrust under
the grill, and a prod with the finger showed them
to be ready, though the cod was not. So the
pressed steak was left cooking while the rest went
underneath to warm.

To reduced stock John now added about a
quarter of a pint of the single cream, and continued
reducing the mixture for a minute or two. Then he
added another ounce of cream together with a
small squeeze of fresh lemon, still reducing.

Why not add more lemon, I asked (because I
like lemon). John said, "I'm a bit nervous about
this cream curdling. Supermarket cream seems
less well-behaved . . ." (His restaurant cream
comes direct from a farm, where the animals have
individual pedigrees and can trace their ancestors
back to the first stirrings of life on this planet, or

so it seems.)

The pasta water was boiling – so in went the *paglia e fieno*. The beans went into the pot vacated by the leeks. And by now that bit of oblong cod had been grilling for twelve minutes and was done: John set it with the trout – a burst of white amongst the angry red.

Another blob of cream went into the reducing sauce, but still John was not happy with the thickness, though almost half a pint had by now been added to the stock. On and on went the reduction.

After two or three minutes of cooking the pasta was ready so he strained it and put in the waiting fried leeks.

The last bit of cream went into the sauce: would he never be satisfied? Would we never eat?

John strained the beans.

Now . . .? Now . . .?

He spooned up some sauce, watching it trickle off the wooden spoon with a fierce eye which seemed to measure viscosity to within the finest degree of whatever one measures viscosity in. It seemed incredibly thick to me.

And yes, John turned finally to the little pile of chopped coriander leaves and tossed them into the sauce, letting them gently simmer for no more than a minute, while plates were laid on the table, and trout fillets doled out together with a bit of the cod.

The sauce was poured. Here was the pasta and leek; here were the beans.

What a meal. The coriander in the sauce was beautifully balanced, despite the risk John had taken by throwing in all the leaves at once (a more cautious soul might have added them little by little to avoid over-flavouring). It was a marvellously dry, deep flavour which mingled perfectly with the texture of the cream and allowed the taste of the trout itself to flourish.

The pasta, aided by leek tasting of olive oil and garlic, had its own charms, and the beans were crisply done.

John said that he was glad he had grilled the

trout fillets, but sorry he had not thought to skin them – which would have helped the stock and left a cleaner plate.

We both tried the frozen cod. It was undeniably good. John nodded and said, "Quite a good flavour. Goes well with the sauce . . ."

We finished the meal in silence, then went on to discuss variations on the theme.

VARIATIONS

Let me start with an admission. John and I were so tickled by the idea of coriander sauce and frozen fish that we tried exactly the same thing on another occasion with two frozen tuna steaks.

They looked marvellous on the packet – thick and pink and succulent. But this turned out to be a credit to the photographer who took the original picture rather than to the fellow with the bandsaw who chopped up the examples we found inside. They were thin and greyish and ragged.

Nonetheless, John went ahead – poaching them this time because tuna has a strong taste and needs less attention to bring out the flavour.

He made the sauce in exactly the same way, cream with coriander. And the meal we sat down to eat was dreadful. The tuna turned out like tough old pork. It was so poor that I was moved to get up halfway through the meal and fry my portion for three more minutes – in vain. Tough old porky stuff it remained.

The moral of this tale is that, though the frozen cod steak was delightful, the same cannot be said of frozen tuna. Perhaps not all frozen tuna, but certainly our pack. Yet I have tried the fish fresh many times with good results. So the best advice I can offer is that, when buying frozen fish in a closed packet, try and open it before you pay. Look at the goods, not the picture.

More constructively, John put his thoughts to what *would* work with a similar sauce: "A good bass," he proposed, "or a really big lump of turbot. And salmon, of course – but nothing oilier than that. None of the cheaper fish, and I don't even think the smaller flat fish would work with this sort of heavy sauce.

"But you *could* use coriander just on its own, with something like sprats or herring or mackerel."

He sketched the meal: pour generous quantities of olive oil into a frying pan with seasalt and a clove of crushed garlic; heat well then add sliced leeks with chopped coriander leaves and stir-fry for two minutes.

Then take out the leeks and coriander and add the fish – herrings, sprats or mackerel – to the same pan and fry quickly, turning once. Now serve the fish, pouring the cooked olive oil over the top and tossing the leeks and coriander on the side as a salad. A great and cheap meal.

Alternatively you could vary the sauce, using a vegetable stock base exactly as described already, but adding cream and then a little fresh ginger at the end instead of coriander. "Make it thinner, though," John warned. "Ginger needs to be *floating* in its medium."

Chopped parsley with the cream would work as well, he said, and so would chives.

More interestingly, John proposed a sauce of Pernod, fennel and butter as an accompaniment to trout fillets or salmon.

For this, you would make a vegetable stock then strain it and reduce the liquid to about half a cup of fluid, having started with under half a pint of water. Then gently melt in about three ounces of butter, adding a small quantity of Pernod and some lemon juice and salt and pepper: "Get that into a good liaison," said John, "then just before serving add a little chopped fennel."

A reminder now of the meal John cooked that day.

TROUT FILLETS IN CREAM AND CORIANDER
Ingredients for 4

1 ½-2 lb (700-900 g) whole fresh trout
or 1-1 ½ lb (450-700 g) fillet
½ pint (275 ml) water
seasalt, black pepper
leek trimmings (for stock) *or* 1 medium onion

few small slivers fresh ginger
1 clove garlic
10-12 leaves fresh coriander
1 oz (25 g) butter
½ pint (275 ml) single cream
squeeze of fresh lemon
(leeks, fresh pasta and green beans were the
accompanying vegetables)

1   Boil a stock containing half a pint of water, a pinch of salt, chopped leek trimmings (or onion), slivers of ginger, one crushed, sliced garlic clove and the stalks of the coriander, also chopped. Put to one side the dozen chopped leaves.

2   After about fifteen minutes, strain the stock and set on a high gas to reduce after tasting and adding more salt and pepper as needed.

3   Meanwhile, dip the trout fillets in a little melted butter and place under a medium grill to cook. These will take about eight minutes to cook.

4   Add half a pint of fresh cream to the reduced stock, a little at a time, plus a few drops of fresh lemon juice. Continue reducing and adding more cream until you have a good, thick sauce.

5   Throw in the sliced coriander leaves (preferably a few at a time, tasting as you do so) and cook for one minute. Then serve.

6   If serving with pasta and leeks, remember to fry the diagonally cut leeks in olive oil and garlic first, then boil the pasta and throw in the cooked leeks at the end.

12

SMOKED COD'S ROE TERRINE WITH TOMATO AND GINGER SAUCE

SALMON FILLETS IN PASTRY WITH SPINACH AND SORREL STUFFING

SALMON STEAKS IN SORREL SAUCE

And so we found ourselves on the last shopping trip, standing outside the fish shop window just as we had done on the first visit, gazing at the goods inside.

I wanted to say something important about how much water had flowed under the bridge since our first meal for this book, but John spotted a decent-looking salmon and went inside and that was my opportunity gone.

And to be honest, there was no time for delay.

This was to be a celebration meal. Within three hours our families and some friends were due to arrive at the restaurant to eat whatever John cooked. There would be seven adults and four children – all looking for something really special on this last occasion. It was a time of much pressure.

John decided that the salmon looked better than the brill next to it and was exactly the right size (just over three pounds in weight) so he went in and bought it. We were launched . . .

Now, while that was being wrapped, he put his mind to the problem of producing a completely different first course, and found the contrast he was seeking in a large moist-looking piece of smoked cod's roe.

This is a product which you must positively want when buying it, because you will never be lured into purchase by looks alone. In shape and colour, smoked cod's roe resembles a gigantic pile of rhinoceros dung. During my days at the shop I found it quite difficult to sell, which is a shame though understandable. Mostly it is bought in order to make that lovely Greek dish taramasalata, (salted grey mullet roe is the alternative basis for that creamy dish), but also it is spooned directly onto bread or biscuits as a starter.

John, buying a three-quarter pound lump which bulged unpromisingly under its taut skin, said that he would *not* be making taramasalata: although what the alternative would be, he had yet to decide. Almost ready to leave now, he added one kipper and a bloater to the menu and we left the shop.

(Kippers and bloaters, by the way, are both smoked herrings. The difference between them is that a kipper is split and gutted and smoked for longer than a bloater, which is lightly cured ungutted and therefore has a more tangy flavour and a firmer texture.)

Wary of time we rushed round to Safeway to pick up a piece of fresh ginger but abandoned all other shopping, relying on the fact that John's

restaurant larder had only just been restocked.

Off we went. Here was the restaurant and a tiny cup of civilising coffee sipped in separate corners of the kitchen while we waited like title-fight boxers for the last great battle to begin. It was eleven o'clock. Finally John opened the shopping bag, took out the whole salmon, and prepared to start work . . .

Or not quite.

At the final second, before knife touched fish, he hesitated, then said, "I was thinking of making some pastry and wrapping the salmon fillets in it, which would be fun . . . but it would be more interesting to do it in two ways: that could look even better on the plate."

How?

"Well, I could fillet it from here on down . . ." The knife made a speculative mark on the salmon skin at a point nine inches from the tail, " . . . and I could wrap those fillets in pastry, and use the top end of the fish to make very thin steaks. With a sauce . . . a sorrel sauce . . ."

Looking at the fish, and at the range of other potential ingredients now spread across the table – smoked cod's roe, bloater, herring, and now some vegetables, here some cream, there some butter – I blanched a little.

Would this be setting too high a standard, I asked, to propose a meal consisting of *two* types of main course, as well as a fishy starter?

John came down with a bump from the clouds of invention. No, he said, it wouldn't. We mulled it over for a while as the seconds ticked away and the Hour of the Relative drew nearer.

Firstly, said John, the job could be very easily achieved without much extra effort; besides, anyone following the idea could simply choose one way or the other if they felt intimidated. It was not essential to do both at once.

Secondly, he said, the effect of one pastry-clad slice of salmon placed alongside a pure oval steak would be impressive, adding a little more interest to the taste and appearance of the meal.

Finally (point made with a flourish, as if

disclosing a winning hand at cards), it provided a useful way out of that old cooking dilemma: what to do with the tail of a salmon once you have cut all the steaks you can reasonably squeeze from the main body? (Salmon tails were another problem in the shop, it is true; we used to have rows of them lined up at the weekend like kittens nobody wanted.)

Under this barrage of logic I could only retreat to my pencil and paper, daring John to complete all these proposed dishes by lunch-time. We would see . . . I hissed; we would see . . .

Here is what happened: First Course, Second Course. Blow by blow.

BASIC PREPARATION

FIRST COURSE: "I'm going to make a terrine out of the roe," said John, "but I'll need to make a sauce to go with it, because it might be a little dry on its own. I think a tomato sauce. Tomato and ginger . . ."

First the skin, which is bitter and rubbery, had to be removed from the roe.

John cut down the centre and took out the insides by a mixture of scraping and peeling, putting the "meat" into a waiting bowl. So many unkind customers in the shop would ask me to do this job for them that under pressure of threatened insanity I found a slightly easier method – using a teaspoon, making firm, scooping strokes, easing up whenever the skin tore. It does work.

With the job done, John spooned the resultant brown mess into a food-processor bowl, adding the following ingredients: a quarter of one garlic clove, crushed and sliced; three dessertspoonfuls of Gordon's gin ("for the flavour . . ." It sounded like an advertisement), three twists of black pepper, six fluid ounces of single cream and two whole eggs.

The Magimix purred contentedly for thirty seconds and then the thick, runny liquid was poured back into a mixing dish.

John now whipped up a further six fluid ounces

of double cream and folded this thick paste into the puréed mixture.

Why not simply put all the cream in at once, before processing?

"It produces a lighter mixture this way," said John, "and besides that, too much whipping could turn the thick cream buttery. This way you have more control."

Those not wanting to buy both single and double cream, he added, could use only the double: but in that case it would be best to beat *all* the cream and fold it in after putting the rest of the ingredients through the processor on their own, in order to avoid the risk of ending up with half a pound of Lurpak.

Now he was tasting the mixture, dipping and licking one finger, declaring that it needed nothing else. He buttered the sides and bottoms of some small ramekins and gently poured some terrine into each.

Do, please, remember two things. The first is that this mixture was thick enough to form small hillocks at a touch. You must be careful when adding your liquid ingredients or it will become too runny.

The second is that you must butter the ramekins well. Even with the coating John applied we later found it difficult to prise each terrine from its mould. We bashed them on the table in the end, and swore; that did it.

John now placed the ramekins into a flat, shallow dish containing half an inch of water (to prevent the terrine from cooking too quickly) and placed this under cover in the oven. The temperature was set at Gas Mark 3 (325°F, 170°C). They took about fifty minutes to cook, but John checked the pots regularly, prodding with his fingers, aiming for a light, moist sponge-like consistency.

In the meanwhile, there was the sauce to prepare.

He began – as so often happens – with a large onion, chopping it then heating the pieces gently with a generous piece of butter in a small pan.

"I've chopped the onion well," said John, "but it's going through the sieve at the end so it doesn't matter too much."

About four minutes later he added three quarters of a pound of ripe tomatoes to the pan ("Don't cut these too small, otherwise the skin might go through the sieve"), together with half a dozen twists of black pepper and two or three thin slivers of fresh ginger. Up went the gas.

Catching sight of one stalk of celery on the side, John grabbed this too, chopped it, and threw it in: "Celery is a wonderful ingredient," he explained. "It keeps for ages and it's always good to have some handy."

What about the hapless folk who have none? What could they use instead?

"Add spices," said John. "Possibly allspice, even cinnamon. Not cloves though, that would be too strong in this sort of quantity. Too risky. The idea is to produce a taste with some breadth and depth – cloves would just dominate."

Twenty-five minutes later – the timing for this sauce is not critical – John sieved the whole mixture, forcing it hard through the mesh using a wooden spoon. The result was a powerful, slightly sweet liquid of ruddy-brown hue. Too close in colour to the cooking terrines which it was to accompany, John decided. So he rummaged amongst the vegetables to unearth some courgettes which he sliced finely into julienne, matchstick shreds then fried in olive oil and garlic, and laid aside to cool.

What, though, of this kipper and this bloater?

Brown and uninspiring they glared at us from the kitchen table, defying all intelligent comment beyond the fact that they were not going to stretch very far – not without filleting. Herrings are not easy creatures to fillet. They are a celebration of bone.

John took the bloater first. Laying the fish on its side he pressed firmly downwards with his left hand then sliced along the backbone with a knife. One good firm slice, blade angled slightly upwards in order to attack the fillet directly under his hand

rather than the one crushed against the chopping board.

This fish has "rib" bones, which the filleter discovers soon after opening up the backbone. Stay calm. Simply follow these outwards with the knife, curving back downwards as you approach the belly. The tail will be simpler to fillet than the top but with a steady hand and steely nerve the meat will eventually come free. Turn the fish over and do the same to the other side.

Remember, no matter how good at this you become, *some* bones will remain, so do not get depressed when one of these later gets stuck in your teeth at the meal table. Spit it out and carry on eating the delicious flesh.

The open kipper is more straightforward, because its frame is already exposed. You simply run the knife under the visible rib bones on either side of the backbone and lift the whole thing clear.

You may find it easier to run your fingers hard up and down the bonework first, pressing the ribs through the flesh, making them easier to identify and pull away.

Having done so, John cut both fish into short strips about half an inch wide. Then, because the gin was still handy, he poured a dessertspoonful into a flat baking tray, added a knob of butter and carefully put in the strips of fish – their skin sides uppermost. He covered the tin with some baking foil and put it in the oven with the terrine for fifteen minutes. This would add a little shape to the first course, he said.

Time plodded on.

SECOND COURSE: The salmon lay before us on the table like a beautiful silver torpedo, the single flaw of a knifemark in its side where John had proposed filleting the tail, steaking the top.

Before any of this could be done, however, the fish had to be headed, cleaned and scaled. The very words take me back to shop days when fine summer mornings would find us doing exactly this to salmon after salmon, an almost endless flow of silver, an exhausting flurry of flying scales and

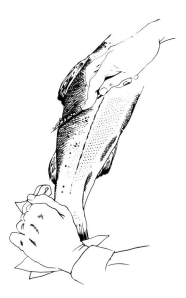

Scaling salmon with a knife, working from tail end – a similar approach can be used for any fish, e.g. bass, red and grey mullet

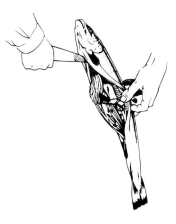

Cutting salmon, working towards head with knife

sordid heaps of bagged-up guts. Fish up to twelve pounds in weight were manhandled up the shop two at a time, thumped onto the preparation table and processed. Sometimes it seemed a pity, such wonderful creatures rendered ugly but usable in such numbers; mostly, though, it was just tiring.

On a memorable occasion I visited the salmon farm in the Outer Hebrides where many of these fish came from. We were taken by motorboat to the caged rafts in the middle of a huge sea loch where the salmon were kept in batches of five thousand. We threw in food and the surface of the water turned cream with frantic activity. They asked me to pick a salmon for myself and when I pointed a six-pound fish was struck once, cleanly on the head with a short wooden club, bagged up and handed over. We cooked it that night in a cottage warmed by peat fires.

John picked up this smaller salmon and began to scale it. Holding it by the tail he firmly rubbed against the scales with a knife, pushing towards the head. The sharp edge of the blade will do for this if you are careful, but do not press down too hard or you will cut and ruin the flesh. Also, John avoided doing this too quickly: real speed would have sent scales flying up to stick on the ceiling.

Now he gutted the fish, prodding the knife into its belly at the rear opening, moving the blade swiftly to the gills, hauling out all the guts and blood. He paid particular attention to the blood channel on the backbone, scraping diligently until it was thoroughly clean (a teaspoon helps with this job; then a dash under the tap).

Finally the head came off with a single slice of the knife just behind the gills – and the salmon was ready for dividing.

Though time was pressing, the business which now followed was restful and pleasing to watch: the conversion of the headless body into perfect pieces of meat.

John separated the nine-inch end piece with one clean cut of his knife. He then filleted this tail by slicing down the backbone on one side (there are no "rib" bones to get in the way at the tail of

the fish) until one whole flap came free, then turning the piece over he simply did the same to the other side.

To skin the bright red fillets, John pressed the knife into the skin through the tail meat and worked it up to the top while pulling the skin down with his left hand.

Taking steaks off the main body he had to be slightly more careful because he wanted slivers rather than thick lumps: the danger is that in cutting so small you squash the meat, so be gentle, especially when reaching the bone, where you will have to increase knife pressure.

Having completed this task, John laid his beautiful shiny steaks on a flat, buttered dish with a little more butter on each piece of fish, covered it with foil and put it in the fridge while he attacked the rest of the meal.

Three things remained to be done: make some shortcrust pastry to wrap round the salmon fillets; prepare a filling for this parcel; and make a sauce for the steaks.

It all seemed too much to do in too little time, and by now I was standing in one corner practising ways of saying "I told you so" without actually thumbing my nose and wiggling my fingers. John, however, seemed undismayed, though the tempo of his work was gradually rising.

He began with the pastry: four ounces of butter sliced into eight ounces of sieved plain flour and mixed with a pinch of salt and – less usually – half a teaspoon of icing sugar. "It improves the texture and adds just a touch of sweetness," said John. Finally, a little water to produce a workable mixture (sometimes he uses milk, cream or an egg instead of water).

Leaving the pastry to rest and develop elasticity before rolling, John turned to the problem of producing a filling to spread between the two salmon tail fillets.

He had already decided to use fresh spinach as the basis for this, mainly because it is one of the few sympathetically flavoured vegetables which will turn into a usable mass when cooked. Now,

recalling that he planned to make sorrel sauce for
the steaks, John decided to bridge the two by
mixing a little sorrel with the spinach as well.

He swiftly chopped a medium onion, throwing
the pieces into a saucepan with a large lump of
butter. Onto a gentle gas now for three to four
minutes while he fell upon half a pound of spinach,
trimming the rough stalks and throwing the leaves
into a bowl with one ounce of trimmed sorrel.

"Sorrel has a lovely sharp, rich flavour which
goes well with almost any fish," John explained.
"It's almost the equivalent of lemon – I sometimes
use it with lemon, to boost it."

Was it difficult for the average cook to get hold
of? He shook his head. "You can sometimes buy
sorrel in shops," he said. "But you can grow it
very easily. Three or four plants in the garden
would give you enough sorrel to make sauce or
soup every week or so from May to October. The
plants last for three years . . ."

Winkling a whole nutmeg from a cupboard,
John now grated a pinch into the cooking onion,
but regretted the fact that there was no mace to
use instead: "Mace is gentler," he said. "But
nutmeg is okay for a small, controlled amount."

With those onion pieces now well-cooked but
clear – not brown – John added a pinch of salt and
threw in the green rain of spinach and sorrel,
stirring then allowing to cook for a further four
minutes. At the end of this time he took it off the
gas, spread it onto the chopping-board and sliced
again and again with a knife until the mess turned
into a fine, usable slurry: tacky on the fingers, of
course, but easier to do at this stage than when
raw.

Now, with minutes pressing, it was time to
roll the pastry into two thin leaves, fleck the base
with tiny points of butter and lay in place the first
salmon fillet.

Fine. A burst of bright red on the pale yellow
pastry, smeared at last with that agricultural-
looking mulch from the chopping-board – sorrel
and spinach – which was then mopped deftly with a
kitchen towel to sop up left-over liquid. The

second fillet was lowered into place to make the sandwich, and the edges of pastry flicked up and pressed in, finally sealed with the additional, top layer of pastry. A brush with milk and water and the triangular-shaped package was levered onto a baking tin and pushed into an oven already warmed by the cooked terrines.

The temperature was raised to Gas Mark 6 (400°F, 200°C) and it was ready in about forty-five minutes – tested several times with a discreetly probing knife which felt for resistance at the centre. Hold the knife blade against your lips after prodding once; see if the meat has warmed it.

All that remained to be done was boil some pasta and green beans and prepare the sorrel sauce. Here though was my wife, horrendously early, smile fading as she was bundled out of the kitchen to clutch a sherry and wait, wait, wait . . .

John finely chopped one ounce of sorrel while heating two dessertspoonfuls of dry vermouth in a small saucepan, together with four fluid ounces of single cream and a couple of twists of black pepper. He raised the temperature under the pan and when the liquid had reduced by simmering he added a further four ounces of double cream (this gave body without the need for quite so much reduction).

Distracted for a moment by a new inrush of friends and relatives, John left the sauce untended for too long, returning with a whoop to find it quietly separating: "This is a disaster! It's like scrambled bloody egg!" A premature cry, as it turned out, for the addition of one judicious egg yolk rescued the situation, leaving John to throw in the sorrel plus a pinch of salt and finish the sauce with a final two minutes of very gentle warming.

People pawed hungrily at the kitchen door. We called out gaily, "It's ready!" We ate on time, and thoroughly on target.

For those of you who will attempt to repeat this entire meal, let me summarise the final result.

In the first course, the terrine was wonderful – strong, salty (salt from the cod's roe) and with a

powerful and warm flavour; the tomato sauce was an important part of this dish, because without it the terrine might have tasted a little dry. Together they were a perfect mixture.

The fillets of kipper and bloater were an interesting side dish but the gin used in their cooking was only faintly discernible: it might be best either to put a little more in or leave it out entirely.

The main course was almost an embarrassment of riches: both the salmon in pastry and the steaks were delicious, and we all found that the sorrel sauce went beautifully with either dish.

Finally, a note about my nine-year-old son, Benjamin, who, during the course of this meal wandered out into the restaurant garden and fell backwards into the sheer-sided, six-foot deep fish pond, causing me to abandon my food rather hastily. Though he took the edge off my appetite, he is alive and well.

VARIATIONS

John's first thoughts were for the smoked cod's roe. "It would have been better to have added a little white fish during the food-processing," he said. "Some plaice or lemon sole fillet – maybe half a pound to go with three quarters of a pound of roe. I think that would have lightened the texture . . ."

A "non-Mediterranean" version of taramasalata would also be worthwhile, he said: something to eat as a dip or a pâté. Using up to half a pound of smoked cod's roe, John would have mixed in half a clove of crushed garlic and five or six fluid ounces of single cream, together with a scattering of breadcrumbs. This should all be food-processed for twenty seconds, he said, before adding a few drops of lemon juice, then stirring and tasting, then adding a little more juice if necessary, and so on.

Using smoked cod's roe as a sauce base would also be effective, particularly to go with salmon fillets or steaks.

For this, you would add one ounce of smoked

cod's roe to about five fluid ounces of single
cream, heating and stirring gently in a saucepan
for one minute then adding about half the quantity
of double cream, a little lemon juice and a small
amount of chopped parsley for colour, heating for
just half a minute more then serving.

A colourful way of using the salmon, said John,
would be to combine it with several layers of
spinach stuffing, made into a terrine. To achieve
this you would first make a basic spinach filling by
cooking a medium onion with a little butter, then
adding half a pound of trimmed spinach leaves and
half a garlic clove (with or without one ounce of
sorrel) and cooking for two minutes. Let it cool,
then add an egg and liquidise with a pinch of grated
nutmeg or mace, plus five fluid ounces of single
cream – adding the cream carefully to avoid
producing a wet mixture: you should be able to
make stiff hillocks on the surface by touching the
liquid.

Now you would take some fillets of salmon –
from the tail-end preferably, as these hold
together better than the flaky meat at the top –
and make lateral cuts to produce thin "sheets" of
meat about a quarter of an inch thick. Line a three-
or four-inch-deep tin with blanched spinach leaves
then put in the terrine and salmon in layers. Cover
and cook in a water bath for about forty-five
minutes, testing regularly to see if it has reached
that damp, bouncy firmness which shows it is
ready.

Finally, the finished terrine would need to be
compressed while cooling: simply arrange a tin on
top, with a pound of sugar or a couple of scale
weights for pressure. But make sure you do this
on a draining-board or in another container, John
warned, because the liquid will overflow as weight
is applied. Also, add the pressure a little at a time
to avoid squashing the food too much: the whole
idea is to make terrine and salmon hold together,
not to produce pancakes.

One last word on terrines in general. To save
last-minute panics they can easily be made one or
two days before you plan to eat them – as can the

sauce. When you plan a particularly complex series of dishes it may be worth getting at least one of them done beforehand.

A less complicated way of varying the salmon and pastry dish would be to tone up the stuffing: leek and orange would be a good alternative, said John. Chop a small onion and cook it with some butter, pepper and very finely chopped leek and some grated orange zest – not juice, or the mixture will become too wet. Season, then mop up excess liquid and spread it onto the salmon fillets.

In the same way, grated lemon and a little sliced ginger would mix beautifully with spinach and onion.

There is, as you will see, very wide scope for personal experiment with this series of dishes (I wrapped the salmon in shop-bought puff pastry and it was marvellous). But if you would like to start with the original meal, here, finally, is a summary of what John did.

SMOKED COD'S ROE TERRINE

Ingredients as a starter for 6-8
– as a main course for 6

10-12 oz (275-350 g) smoked cod's roe

end of garlic

3 dessertspoonfuls gin

pepper

6 fl oz (175 ml) single cream

6 fl oz (175 ml) double cream

(or 12 fl oz (350 ml) double cream)

2 eggs

butter

1   Skin the cod's roe and food-process for thirty seconds with the end of (crushed) garlic, the gin, pepper, single cream and eggs.

2   Whip a further six fluid ounces of double cream and fold this into the mixture.

3   Pour the mixture into some buttered ramekins, place in a water-bath, cover and cook for about fifty minutes at Gas Mark 3 (325°F, 170°C). Test frequently.

4   Allow to cool before scraping round the edges with a knife and tapping out onto plate.

TOMATO AND GINGER SAUCE

1 medium onion
knob of butter
12 oz (350 g) tomatoes
pepper
3 slivers fresh ginger
1 stalk celery

1   Chop the onion and heat gently with some butter for three to four minutes.

2   Add the chopped tomatoes plus six twists of pepper, two or three slivers of ginger and a chopped celery stalk.

3   Cook for up to twenty minutes until well mixed. Press through a sieve, scraping bottom of sieve with wooden spoon.

SALMON FILLETS IN PASTRY WITH SPINACH AND SORREL STUFFING
Ingredients as a starter for 6-8
– as a main course for 6

1 ½-2 lb (700-900 g) tail-end of salmon
(or a 2lb (900 g) plus whole fish)
1 medium onion
knob of butter
½ lb (225g) fresh spinach
1 oz (25 g) sorrel
pinch grated nutmeg

For pastry:
4 oz (110 g) butter
8 oz (225 g) plain flour

pinch salt
½ teaspoon icing sugar
water

1   Make the pastry – it can be resting while you
     prepare the other ingredients: mix the butter with
     the sieved plain flour, pinch of salt, half a teaspoon
     of icing sugar, and finally, a little water.

2   Fillet and skin the salmon tail.

3   For the stuffing, chop a medium onion and heat
     gently for four to five minutes with a large lump of
     butter.

4   Add the trimmed spinach and sorrel leaves, with a
     pinch of nutmeg. Stir and cook for four more
     minutes.

5   Remove from gas. Cool and chop the mixture.

6   Roll the pastry into two thin sheets, dot the base
     layer with butter, add one fillet of salmon. Fill with
     the stuffing, add the second piece of salmon. Wrap
     with pastry and trim.

7   Brush with milk and water. Place on a floured tin.
     Bake in a pre-heated oven for about forty-five
     minutes at Gas Mark 6 (400°F, 200°C). Test
     regularly with a knife.

SALMON STEAKS IN SORREL SAUCE

Ingredients as a starter for 6-8
– as a main course for 6

1½-2 lb (700-900 g) top end salmon

butter

2 dessertspoonfuls dry vermouth

4 fl oz (110 ml) single cream

4 fl oz (110 ml) double cream

(or 8 fl oz (220 ml) of either)

1 egg yolk

1 oz (25 g) sorrel

salt, black pepper

This sauce can also be used with the salmon in pastry.

1   Cut the steaks into quarter-pound portions. They will take about fifteen minutes to cook with a little butter, covered in a medium oven.

2   Heat the vermouth with the single cream and two twists of pepper.

3   Reduce by simmering then add the double cream, stir, add one egg yolk. Warm gently, but do not let it boil.

4   After seven or eight minutes, when the sauce seems quite thick, throw in the finely chopped sorrel leaves for a further two minutes cooking. Serve.

INDEX

Figures in italics refer to illustrations